MODERN WORLD NATIONS

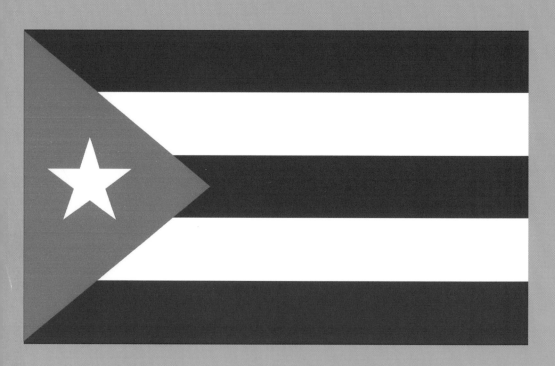

MODERN WORLD NATIONS

Cuba

Richard A. Crooker

Kutztown University

Series Consulting Editor

Charles F. Gritzner

South Dakota State University

CHELSEA HOUSE
PUBLISHERS

A Haights Cross Communications Company

Frontispiece: Flag of Cuba

Cover: The parking lot of the capitol building in Havana is lined with classic American cars. Visitors to Cuba often comment on the many old cars in pristine condition—a consequence of having no U.S. car imports for decades.

CHELSEA HOUSE PUBLISHERS

VP, NEW PRODUCT DEVELOPMENT Sally Cheney
DIRECTOR OF PRODUCTION Kim Shinners
CREATIVE MANAGER Takeshi Takahashi
MANUFACTURING MANAGER Diann Grasse

Staff for CUBA

EDITOR Lee Marcott
PRODUCTION EDITOR Jaimie Winkler
PICTURE RESEARCHER Pat Holl
COVER AND SERIES DESIGNER Takeshi Takahashi
LAYOUT 21st Century Publishing and Communications, Inc.

A Haights Cross Communications ✈ Company

http://www.chelseahouse.com

First Printing

1 3 5 7 9 8 6 4 2

Library of Congress Cataloging-in-Publication Data

Crooker, Richard A.
  Cuba / Richard A. Crooker, Charles F. Gritzner.
    p. cm. -- (Modern world nations)
Includes bibliographical references and index.
  ISBN 0-7910-6932-X
  1. Cuba--Juvenile literature. I. Gritzner, Charles F. II. Title. III.
Series.
  F1758.5 .C75 2002
  972.91--dc21
                              2002007328

Table of Contents

Cuba

Villages along the coast of Cuba overlook the lagoons, coral reefs, bays, and beaches of the Caribbean Sea.

Introducing Cuba

C uba is an alligator-shaped island and the largest country in the Caribbean Sea. It is located just south of the Tropic of Cancer (23½° north latitude). Florida lies just 90 miles (145 kilometers) to the north and the Yucatán Peninsula of Mexico is to the west. Cuba is one of the Caribbean region's Greater Antilles, a chain of islands that in addition to Cuba consists of Hispaniola (which includes the countries of Haiti and the Dominican Republic), Puerto Rico, and Jamaica.

Cuba has a varied landscape, fertile limestone soils, and a semitropical climate, making the island ideal for agriculture. Quaint fishing villages, colonial architecture, coral reefs, emerald lagoons, wave-cut sea cliffs, lush mangrove forests, limestone caves, and sun-drenched beaches combine to form one of the most inviting islands in the Caribbean region. Christopher Columbus visited Cuba on his first voyage to the New World in 1492. The island's physical beauty and potential riches charmed him, and he claimed the island for Spain.

Cuba's location is strategically important because it straddles maritime approaches to the Atlantic Ocean, the Gulf of Mexico, and the Caribbean Sea. Whoever controls Cuba controls sea-lanes passing between these bodies of water. The Spaniards were quick to recognize Cuba as a gateway between the Atlantic and the Gulf of Mexico. Control of Cuba, they reasoned, would give them control of the sea-lanes to a colonial empire in the New World. Spanish conquistadors (conquerors) used Cuba as a fortress and as a jumping-off point for the conquest of Mexico and for expeditions into North America.

In modern times, Cuba has been important to the United States because of its gateway location. American interest in Cuba's location contributed to the start of the Spanish-American War (1898). Following Cuba's independence from Spain in 1902 until the end of the Cuban Revolution in 1959, the island's proximity to U.S. markets for tropical crops and their products attracted huge agricultural investments from American businesses. Moreover, due to Cuba's proximity to the United States, the island became a vacation resort for wealthy Americans and a haven for Americans seeking such illegal pastimes as gambling and prostitution.

Since 1959, under Castro's iron-fist Communist dictatorship, Cuba's strategic location became a centerpiece of the Cold War. The Cold War (1945-1991) was a war of hostile diplomacy, intrigue, and subversion between Communist and non-Communist countries. These countries tried to gain political victories over each other without actually going to war. The former Soviet Union was Communist and saw Cuba as a base for military and espionage operations because of its proximity to the United States.

The Cold War's focus on Cuba's strategic location resulted in a series of significant events, including a U.S. trade embargo, an

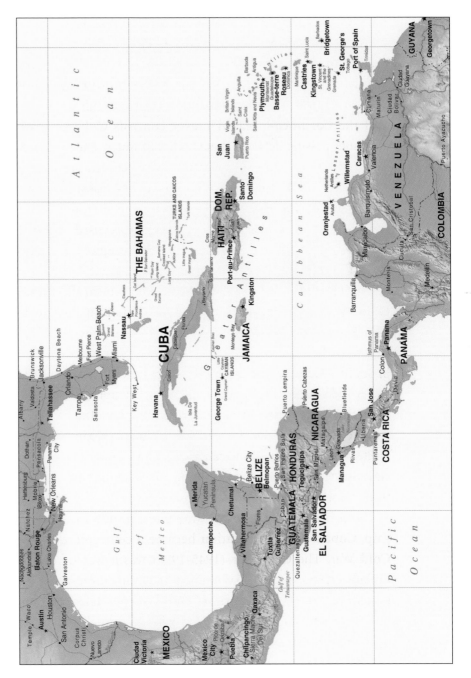

Cuba is an alligator-shaped island and the largest country in the Caribbean Sea. It is located just south of the Tropic of Cancer. Florida lies just 90 miles (145 kilometers) to the north and the Yucatán Peninsula of Mexico is to the west.

Sugarcane is harvested in Cuba from January through April. This fieldworker uses oxen to carry the cane from the field.

ill-fated U.S.-backed invasion of Cuba, and the Cuban missile crisis. Today, Cuba is politically and economically isolated from the United States, even though Havana, the capital, is the major Latin American city closest to the United States. Neither country has an embassy in the other's capital. Most Americans cannot travel to Cuba, and American businesses cannot trade with Cuba, except under special circumstances.

Cuba stands out among nations in several ways, aside from its strategic location. The island was Spain's last colony in the Western Hemisphere. It had the first passenger railroad in Latin America. Cuba was the first country in Latin America to have a radio broadcasting station. Its citizens were the first people outside of the United States to play baseball.

Cuba is also the largest island country in the Caribbean Sea. It is the 16th largest island in the world. It has the largest population among the Caribbean countries. It is home to the smallest species of bird and the largest species of cactus in the world. Cuba became the first country in the Western

Hemisphere to embrace Communism. It is the only country with a Communist government in the region today. The island's main trading partners are Russia and Spain. Its most important money-making crop is sugarcane. Its most famous product is the cigar.

Additionally, Cuba's leader, President Fidel Castro, is one of the most recognizable world leaders. Until recently, the tall, bearded Castro, who likes to dress in combat boots and fatigues, has held his country closely to the ideals of Communism. Strict Communism requires that the State own all businesses. In recent years, Castro has loosened his hold slightly to allow some privately owned Cuban businesses as well as investments from non-Communist countries.

Castro, who became 76 years old on August 13, 2002, has held power for more than 40 years. No dictator, viceroy, or any other head of state in Latin America has endured for so long. Indeed, Castro has been in power longer than any current head of state in the world, except for King Bhumibol Adulyadej of Thailand and Queen Elizabeth II of the United Kingdom and the British Commonwealth of Nations.

It is likely that the aging Castro will retire from or die in office within the next few years. When he is gone from the scene, Cuban experts think that Cuba will undergo major political and economic reforms. However, they cannot predict for sure what these reforms will be like or what Cuba will be like in the future. Nevertheless, a better understanding of Cuba today will help prepare for a better understanding of Cuba tomorrow.

Spain built fortifications, such as this one at the harbor of Santiago de Cuba, to protect the island from invaders. Today, Santiago de Cuba is a mining and shipping center.

2

Physical Landscapes

The Islands

Although we often speak of Cuba as one island, Cuba is actually an archipelago, or group of islands, whose total combined area is 42,803 square miles (110,860 square kilometers). Cuba is the largest island in this archipelago, making up 95 percent of the total land area of the archipelago. The second largest island, the Isla de Juventud (Island of Youth) is 864 square miles (2,230 square kilometers), which is about 2 percent of Cuba's total land area. There are about 1,600 additional islands called islets (small rocky islands) and cays (low coral islands). Small archipelagos of cays make up most of the remaining 3 percent of Cuba.

The country's total area is almost identical to that of Ohio. However, Cuba's shape is very different: Ohio is compact, Cuba is elongated and narrow. Cuba curves east and west, and stretches approximately 780 miles (1,250 kilometers), which is the distance between New York City and Chicago. The narrow width varies from 25 to 120 miles (40 to 195 kilometers).

Cuba lays astride principal maritime approaches to the Atlantic Ocean, the Gulf of Mexico, and the Caribbean Sea. These approaches are the Straits of Florida to the north, the Windward Passage to the east, and the Yucatán Channel to the west. These narrow waterways (straits) have played key roles in the history of Cuba. For example, when Cuba was a Spanish colony, Spanish fleets carrying gold and other precious cargo were vulnerable to attack as they converged on the straits. As a result, in the late 16th century Spain built heavy fortifications around Cuba's harbors, so that the fleets could seek protection as well as supplies. More recently, the narrowness of the straits of Florida has encouraged an exodus of Cubans on rickety boats and rafts to the United States.

Submarine Plateau and Rock Types

Geologically, most of Cuba is an exposed portion of an undersea plateau. A plateau is a mass of rock with an elevated table-like surface. Limestone, or calcium carbonate, is the most common rock on the plateau. It is a sedimentary rock created from the cementing of shells of dead sea-dwelling organisms. Most of these organisms are tiny plankton, single-celled organisms that float near the surface of the ocean when they are alive. As they die, their remains (sediments) slowly settle to the bottom of the ocean where they harden into thick layers of limestone. In addition to limestone, Cuba has thin layers of other sedimentary rocks, including sandstone, shale, and mudstone. These rocks formed from depositing and hardening of sand, silt, and clay sediments washed into the sea from continents.

Seafloor deposition created all of these sedimentary rocks between 15 million and 130 million years ago. The rocks

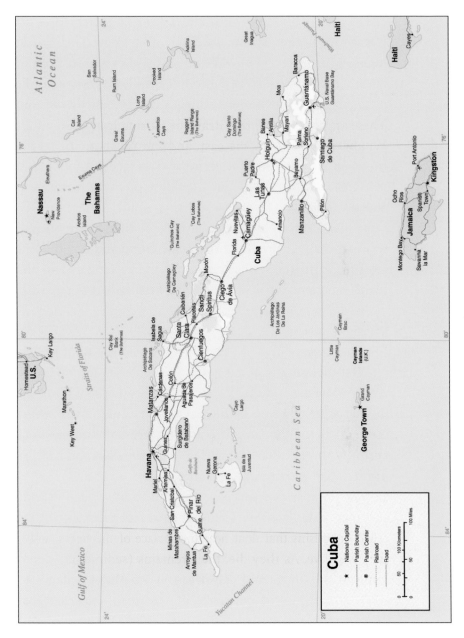

Cuba is a group of islands, which is called an archipelago. The island of Cuba is the largest one, with 95 percent of the country's land area. The second largest island is the Isla de Juventud. There are about 1,600 additional islets that make up the remaining 3 percent of the land area. Cuba is the size of Ohio, but its shape is elongated and narrow and stretches nearly 780 miles (1,250 kilometers).

rested as horizontal layers on the bottom of the sea. The sea was between the North American and Central American lithospheric plates. (Lithospheric plates are large sections of Earth's rocky outer layer.) About 12 million years ago, the plates began moving toward each other—the North American plate moved toward the southwest and the Central American plate toward the northeast. The converging plates forced the rocks on the seafloor between them to rise gradually as a platform and to expose Cuba. Folding, faulting, volcanism, and earthquakes accompanied this uplift. Consequently, Cuba's land surface does not have the flatness of an ancient seafloor. Geologists believe that plate convergence and uplift are still in progress, as occasionally the eastern end of the island experiences powerful earthquakes.

Karst

One of the extraordinary aspects of Cuba's landforms is its karst topography. Karst is the Slavic name of a limestone area in Slovenia, a country in Eastern Europe. Geologists use this term to describe landforms of limestone areas where most or all of the drainage occurs through underground channels and peculiar surface features. Cuba has some of the world's most picturesque karst landscapes.

Karst topography forms wherever acid in surface streams or groundwater dissolves soft limestone. Sinkholes (*hoyos*) are saucer-shaped depressions where surface water collects, sinks, and disappears as groundwater. The acid water filters down from the sinkholes and dissolves the limestone beneath to create underground networks of streams. These streams dissolve more limestone to form cave systems.

Caverns are the largest caves. Sometimes roofs of caverns become fragile and collapse, leaving enclosed basins (*poljes*). When several caverns close to each other collapse, they create large, flat-bottomed depressions with only steep-sided, cone-shaped hills (*mogotes*) left standing. Cotilla Caverns, about

15 miles (24 kilometers) southeast of Havana, are probably the most frequently visited caves in Cuba.

Caverns in Cuba are attractive to tourists because of their natural beauty. However, speleologists (people who study caves) have not adequately explored most of the island's caves. Moreover, people have abused many of them. For example, Cuba's military uses many of the largest caverns to store armaments, explosives, and chemical products. Additionally, agricultural and industrial enterprises discharge tons of wastewater into many caves and sinkholes. Ranchers even use some caves to dispose of dead cattle. These practices not only destroy the beauty of the caves, but they also threaten sensitive habitats of plants and animals, and they pollute the groundwater that travels through the caves.

Limestone Plain

Limestone forms a rolling lowland plain that covers about 60 percent of the island's surface. The plain begins at the base of the Sierra Maestra (a mountain range on the east end of the island), narrows as it arcs north of the foothill town of Santa Clara, and ends at the base of the Sierra de los Organos (a mountain range on the west end of the island). The plain is not perfectly level. To the north, stepped limestone terraces descend quickly toward knifed-edged sea cliffs. To the south, the plain slopes gently toward the soft contours of beaches and mangrove swamps.

Low hills of hard igneous and metamorphic rocks break up the plain in several places. Low, steep-sided hills of limestone are also present. The Zapata Peninsula, with its many lagoons, lakes, and swamps, is also a distinctive lowland feature.

Mountains

About 25 percent of Cuba's surface is mountainous. The pressure of colliding plates created the mountains. Compression causes two general types of mountains: folded

Forests grow in isolated hilly and mountainous regions. The different types of trees are sought for use as building materials and for firewood.

and fault-block. Compression created folded mountains in Cuba when the horizontal layers of sedimentary rock on the bottom of the sea gave in to pressure of converging plates: up-folds became ridges, down-folds valleys. Imagine hands moving together on a flat tablecloth; this movement creates compression and the tablecloth folds into "ridges" and "valleys." Compression and folding of Earth's surface occur in a similar manner.

Compression also caused huge blocks of rock on either side of faults (breaks in Earth's crust) to move up or down, creating fault-block mountains. Magma (molten rock formed deep inside Earth) moved into the faults and onto the surface and cooled to form various types of igneous (volcanic) rocks in the mountains.

There are three mountainous areas in Cuba. Eastern Cuba has the highest mountains, which include the Sierra Maestra and the Baracoa massif. (A massif is a very rugged elevated area composed of numerous mountain ranges.) The Sierra Maestra is a fault-block mountain range that rises steeply out of the sea. Many dark-colored volcanic rocks make up this range. The Sierra Maestra includes Cuba's highest peak, Pico Turquino, which rise about 6,576 feet (2,005 meters) above sea level. This magnificent peak provides a view of the Caribbean Sea to the south and on a clear night, lights glimmering across the Windward Passage in Haiti are visible.

At the very eastern end of the island is the Baracoa massif. The massif's highest summits, which are in the impressive Sierra de Cristal mountain range, rise to about 4,000 feet (1,200 meters). Geologically, the Baracoa massif is a mixture of both folding and faulting. It is made mostly of igneous rock. A narrow valley separates Sierra Maestra and the Baracoa massif. This valley serves as a transportation corridor connecting agricultural towns in the broad Cuato River lowland with coastal ports situated on the eastern end of the island.

The second mountainous area is in central Cuba, south of the city of Santa Clara. Traveling south from Santa Clara, there are low, parallel limestone ridges in which many caves and other karst phenomena have developed. Still farther south, at the edge of Cuba's south shore, is the Sierra del Escambray. This fault-block mountain range dominates the area. Its erosion-resistant summits rise to about 3,500 feet (1,100 meters).

The third mountainous area, Cordillera de Guaniguanico,

which is in the western end of the island, includes two mountain ranges—Sierra del Rosarío and Sierra de los Organos. The highest summit, which is in Sierra de los rganos, is Pico Grande at about 3,000 feet (900 meters) in elevation. However, most elevations in both mountain ranges are well below that height. Despite the lower elevations, the western mountains are very picturesque because of their highly developed karst features.

Throughout Cuba's history, gold, manganese, nickel, chromium, and iron ore have been mined from its mountains. Because of their rugged terrain, these same mountains have also served as safe havens for the many peoples who arrived on Cuba's shores seeking a new home. For example, before Europeans arrived, successive waves of Indians from other regions invaded Cuba. Each time a new group of invaders arrived on the island, some of the Indians who preceded the invaders managed to flee into the mountains. The same dispersal happened when the Spanish arrived. Additionally, when Fidel Castro began his successful revolt against the Cuban government, he used the Sierra Maestra as his main base of operations.

Coastline Features

Cuba's coastline has reefs, cays, and beaches. These three features come from remains of coral polyps (invertebrate animals). Coral polyps are tiny animals that live together in colonies in warm, shallow seawater. When they die, their lime skeletons stay behind to build reefs made of limestone. Coral reefs are hazardous to ships, because they lurk just beneath the ocean surface most of the time (some reefs are exposed at low tide). The remains of an immense number of coral polyps make up a single coral reef. Reefs fringe most of Cuba's coastline, making it dangerous for unwary sailors.

Over time, coral reefs can grow so large that they become low islands or cays. People living in Florida call such islands "keys" as in the Florida Keys. The Camagüey archipelago, which runs parallel to the main island's north-central coastline, is Cuba's largest cay. Other prominent archipelagos made of low coral islands include Sabana and Canarreos.

Sand grains from skeletons of dead coral polyps make up most of Cuba's beaches. Ocean waves break up coral colonies growing on offshore reefs and wash grains of coral sand—and lesser amounts of broken clam and snail shells and sea urchin remains—onto the beaches. The sun bleaches the tiny pieces of coral and other organisms white, giving most of the island's beaches a white-powder texture. The only major exceptions to Cuba's coral beaches are small, black-sand beaches that hug the southern coastline of the Sierra Maestra. These beaches form from the weathering and erosion of igneous rocks that make up the mountain ranges.

Lagoons, sea cliffs, gulfs, and bays account for irregularities in Cuba's coastline. A lagoon is a semienclosed, shallow body of water that lies between the mainland and offshore reefs and islands. The reefs and islands protect the lagoon from the ocean's strong currents and large waves. Lagoons are unique ecosystems for several interrelated reasons. Lagoon waters are brackish, or a mixture of freshwater from streams and saltwater from the sea. Many plants and animals flourish in quiet lagoon waters, such as coral and sea grass. Their presence supports a complex food chain that supports different kinds of animals, such fish, crabs, sea urchins, snails, and clams. Some ocean fish use the semienclosed lagoon when they are very young for protection from predators in the open ocean.

Lagoons were important to the food supply of Indians and early Spanish settlers. They are also an important natural resource to Cubans. Unfortunately, due to overexploitation, important sources of food—fish, turtles, and lobsters—are rare now in some lagoons. Additionally, the government does not have strict pollution laws. As a result, streams drain deadly chemicals from agricultural fields, industrial plants, and sewage into the lagoons.

Sea cliffs exist where the land rises steeply out of the ocean. Waves meet Cuba's limestone shores head-on, where the force of their constant pounding makes indentations that eventually form steep rock pinnacles and sea caves. Sea cliffs make up most of the island's rugged northern shore, usually dropping more than 100 feet (30 meters) to the sea. The southern coastline has more lowland swamps and beaches than the northern coastline does. The only major exceptions are the southern edges of the Sierra del Escambray and the Sierra Maestra. These mountains have prominent sea cliffs and terraces, because they rise out of the sea.

Gulfs are the largest coastal indentations. Gulfs do not make good harbors because their openings are too wide to protect ships from storms. Cuba has three main gulfs: Bataban, Ana María, and Guacanayabo. All three align along the island's southern coast. Bays are smaller indentations than gulfs. Many of Cuba's bays are pouch-shaped ports with very narrow openings that expand into spacious sheltered waters. They serve as safe harbors for ships because their bottleneck openings keep out the ocean's storm waves. Many of Cuba's quaint fishing villages, popularized by Ernest Hemingway's book *The Old Man and the Sea*, are located around harbors. Most of the larger harbors are located on the northern coast, such as Mariel, Havana, Cárdenas, Bahía Honda, Matanzas, and Neuvitas. Large harbors on the southern coast include Guantánamo, Santiago de Cuba, Cienfuegos, and Trinidad.

Climate

Climatologists (scientists who study climate) classify Cuba's climate as tropical because it has year-round high temperatures. Nevertheless, the temperatures are mild considering the country's closeness to the equator.

Cuba's temperatures are mild because of the surrounding ocean's influence. In summer, the ocean cools the island by absorbing and storing a lot of the energy it receives from the sun, rather than releasing it into the air. During Cuba's warmest months, May through October, the average high temperature is a moderately warm 89°F (32°C) for tropical latitudes. In Cuba's coolest months, November through April, the ocean warms the island by releasing solar heat it stored during the summer. As a result, the average low temperature is a pleasant 65°F (19°C). However, in the winter, waves of cold air from North America, which Cubans called *el nortes* (the north winds), may lower individual thermometer readings around Havana to near 40°F (4°C). Occasionally, storms and heavy seas accompany the north winds along the island's northwest coast.

Mean annual rainfall is 40-45 inches (102-114 centimeters). Cuba's primary source of moisture is the trade winds. These winds pick up and bring moisture from the sea to the land. They blow across the island from the northeast and east. Cuba's mountains block the winds and force them to rise, cool, and form clouds. As a result, mountain areas receive more rain than areas downwind from them do. "Rain shadow" is the name given to the drier downwind areas. For example, Guantánamo Bay receives only 24 inches (61 centimeters) of rainfall, because it is in the rain shadow of the Baracoa massif, located north and east of the bay. The massif, facing the wind, receives more than 70 inches (179 centimeters).

The trade winds distribute rainfall unevenly through the year. Typically, 75 percent of the rain occurs during the warmer months (May through October), when the trade winds blow continually toward Cuba. During the "cool" season (November through March), they weaken and deliver less moisture to the island. The wet-summer trade winds are not always a dependable supplier of moisture. They weaken periodically and cause droughts that can last for several years. The most recent drought occurred in 1997-2000 and caused dramatic declines in production of Cuba's major agricultural products: sugar, tobacco, citrus, and coffee.

Tropical Storms and Hurricanes

Tropical storms and hurricanes add to Cuba's rainfall totals about every two years. A tropical storm is weaker than a hurricane. Wind speeds for tropical storms are between 35 and 73 miles per hour (56 and 118 kilometers per hour). When wind speeds exceed 74 miles per hour (118 kilometers per hour), the tropical storm becomes a hurricane. Only about 10 percent of tropical storms in the Atlantic and Caribbean region grow to become hurricanes.

Hurricane season runs from June through November, with the worst storms occurring in September through November. Most hurricanes originate south of Cuba in the Caribbean Sea, or southeast of the island in the Atlantic Ocean. The island of Cuba sits in the paths of storms originating in both areas. Coastal cities, towns, and villages are most vulnerable. Because of its size and elongated east-west shape, hurricanes strike Cuba more often than any other island in the Caribbean and Gulf of Mexico region. Hurricanes affect western Cuba more frequently than eastern Cuba. For example, hurricanes from 1870 to 2001 hit directly or brushed Havana in western Cuba 29 times and Manzanillo in eastern Cuba only 13 times.

Many hurricanes have caused serious damage and deaths in Cuba. The deadliest storm killed an estimated 3,000 people in western Cuba in June 1791. Another storm hit the island in October 1870 killing about 2,000 people. Despite their significance as Cuba's two most deadly storms, they are unnamed, as hurricanes were not given names until 1950. In October 1963, Hurricane Flora, this island's third most deadly storm, hit eastern Cuba with winds up to 120 miles per hour (190 kilometers per hour). This storm killed an estimated 1,000 people and destroyed the country's entire sugar crop.

In recent years, early warnings based on satellite technology have prevented the high death tolls exacted by the storms mentioned previously. For example, in November 2001, Hurricane

Michelle, packing heavy rains and winds in excess of 135 miles per hour (220 kilometers per hour) bombarded Cuba. In Havana, which caught the edge of the storm, Michelle destroyed nearly 200 homes and badly damaged over 35 schools. Throughout western and central Cuba, the storm wiped out more than 1,000 homes. Despite this extensive damage, the storm killed only five people due to early warnings by weather forecasters.

Plants and Animals

Cuba has no physical connection to a continental land-mass. Therefore, wind, migratory birds, and ocean currents carried all life to the islands before the arrival of humans. Settlers who came to Cuba also brought plants and animals to the islands, usually intentionally, sometimes accidentally.

The island has one of the world's richest collections of flowering plants. Botanists (scientists who study plants) estimate that more than 8,000 different species of plants and nearly 2,000 species of animals survive in the island's forests, savannas (grasslands), and coastal waters. More than 3,000 plants and about 170 animals are endemic to the island, meaning they exist in Cuba and nowhere else. Endemic plants and wildlife came early to Cuba and lived there long enough to gradually change and become very different from their ancestors. Only two other islands have more endemic species of plants and animals than Cuba—New Guinea and Madagascar.

Forests cover 24 percent of the island, but they once covered 60 percent of its area. During the 18th and 19th centuries, owners of large landholdings cut down most of the island's tree cover to make room for crop cultivation and livestock grazing. The remaining forest tends to be in relatively remote areas. There are four major forest types in Cuba: semideciduous, mangrove, pine, and tropical rainforest.

Semideciduous forests account for 50 percent of Cuba's remaining forest cover. They are composed of a mixture of broadleaf evergreen and broadleaf deciduous trees. Most of these forests are scattered in isolated areas of hills and mountains. The mangrove forest is the second largest forest type in Cuba; it makes up 33 percent of Cuba's forestland. Mangrove forests grow next to the sea. They are especially concentrated on edges of mudflats that fringe bays, river mouths, banks of tidal lakes, and coastal swamps. The largest mangrove area is in the swamps of the Zapata Peninsula.

The pine forest is the third largest forest type. It accounts for 14 percent of the island's forestland. Some of Cuba's pine trees grow best above 4,265 feet (1,300 meters) in cool temperatures. The oak tree is a companion of the pine tree in this mountainous environment. Mountain peasants depend heavily on pine and oak trees for firewood and building material.

The tropical rainforest is Cuba's fourth and smallest forest type, making up only 3 percent of the island's forest land. Broadleaf evergreen trees form a dense multistoried canopy. Shade-tolerant ferns, orchids, and bromeliads grow beneath the canopy. Small stands of this forest barely survive today in lower elevations of remote mountainous areas. Yet, even now, furniture makers seek out several hardwood tree species—mahogany, ebony, and tropical cedar—in these vanishing forests.

Savannas are tropical grasslands. Rural Cubans use the name that the Arawak Indians gave to these areas, *sabana*, meaning "treeless land," rather than savanna for these areas. Like Cuba's forests, savannas were much more widespread before the arrival of Spaniards. They accounted for about 26 percent of Cuba's original vegetation cover. Savanna grasses now grow in many areas where poor agricultural practices have changed rich forest soils into hardpan soils. (Hardpan soils block roots of trees from penetrating into the ground.) Scattered in the savanna are various species of cacti and palms, including the royal palm. Cuba's savanna grasses thrive in a climate with pronounced wet and dry seasons. The grasses also grow well in freshly burned areas. So for hundreds of years, people have used fire to burn areas where trees would ordinarily grow in order to feed grazing animals.

Palms are members of Cuba's forests and savannas. They are intriguing plants. They can be either a tree or a shrub and usually have a single woody trunk and large, evergreen, feather-like, or fan-shaped leaves growing in a bunch at the top. Cuba has 30 palm species. The palm trees that are associated with savanna soils include the medium-height *cana* palm and the tall *barrigona* palm. Cubans call the *barrigona* palm the big-belly palm because of its distinctive bulge about midway up its truck.

The stately, fast-growing royal palm tree reaches about 130 feet (40 meters) and grows throughout the island's limestone plain. It is easy to identify, because of its slender, silver-gray trunk and crown of dark green fronds. The royal palm is the symbol of Cuba. It occupies the central position in Cuba's national coat of arms and symbolizes strength. Peasant farmers use the bark of the royal palm to make the walls of their *bohiós*, or dwellings, and they use the tree's fronds as roof thatching.

Rural folk use fibers that encircle fruit pods of the majestic *ceiba* (silk-cotton tree) to stuff mattresses, life preservers, and sleeping bags. This huge tree is sacred to many tropical people. Although surrounding trees may be cut away, the mighty ceiba is almost always spared.

Xerophytes (from the Latin for "dry plant") cover about one percent of Cuba's landscape. These plants grow mainly in deserts. However, rain shadow areas of mountains and dry savannas also have them. The coastal terraces in the rain shadow area of the Sierra Maestra and around Guantánamo Bay are the driest areas in Cuba. Various types of cacti and agaves are common there. The most notable cactus is the tree-size *Dendrocereus nudiflorus*, the largest cactus in the world. Dry land soils in Las Villas Province and rain shadow areas in eastern Cuba harbor this special cactus.

Some coastal terraces in Cuba have dry climates. This is an aerial view of such a landscape around Guantánamo Bay in southern Cuba. The bay area is the site of a U.S. naval base.

As with plants, a huge variety of species marks Cuba's animal population. The island has 7,000 species of insects, 4,000 of mollusks, 500 of edible fish, and 300 of birds. There are only a few mammals, however. Most of the wild land animals live in the least disturbed areas—in mangrove swamps of the Zapata Peninsula, in mountainous areas, and on offshore islands.

There are only a few native mammals in Cuba. The *jutía*, or cane rat, is on the brink of extinction. This edible rodent weighs as much as 10 pounds (4 kilograms). People have hunted it to near extinction. A small number of jutía hide out in forest preserves and mangrove-covered cays. The *almiquí* is also in danger of extinction. It is a cat-sized native mammal and resembles a mole. The few almiquí that remain survive in Cuba's eastern mountains. Bats live in Cuba's many limestone caves. People living near the caves collect the bat's droppings (guano) from cave floors and use the droppings as fertilizer.

Reptiles are the most numerous representatives of land animals. The Cuban crocodile is a species of crocodile that only lives in Cuba's freshwater swamps on the Zapata Peninsula and on the Isle de Juventud. The American crocodile outnumbers the Cuban crocodile in these areas. (The American crocodile also lives along the shorelines of all Central American and Caribbean islands and in Florida.) Other reptiles include iguanas, salamanders, 15 poisonous snakes, and a 13-foot (4-meter) long nonpoisonous snake called the *majá de Santa María*. The majá (which means nonpoisonous snake) is Cuba's largest snake.

About 350 species of birds live in Cuba. Year-round inhabitants include varieties of hawks, hummingbirds, owls, parrots, pelicans, quails, spoonbills, and woodpeckers. Cuba boasts the world's smallest bird, the bee hummingbird, which lives primarily in the mangrove swamps of the Zapata Peninsula. This tiny bird is slightly larger than a grasshopper.

Cuba is also a meeting ground for migratory birds from both the tropical zone in northern South America and temperate zones in North America. Migratory birds—including various warblers and thrushes, flamingoes, and herons, and the Cuban trogon—use Cuba as a stopover. Even though it is not a permanent resident of their island, Cubans chose the trogon as their national bird, because it has red, white, and blue feathers, the colors of the Cuban flag.

Havana-born writer and political activist José Martí sacrificed his life for Cuba's independence from Spain. This monument to him is in Cienfuegos, a major seaport and sugar trading center on the south-central coast.

3

Cuba
Through Time

Indians of Cuba

The Siboney and Guanahatabey Indians are the earliest known inhabitants of Cuba. They arrived there sometime after 3500 B.C.E. Both groups lived in small temporary settlements. Their dwellings were concentrated near the ocean, because sea life was their main source of food. They gathered clams, mussels, crabs, and lobsters; hunted manatees and sea turtles; and fished. They also collected wild nuts and fruits and hunted and trapped iguanas, snakes, and birds.

Warlike Arawak Indians began arriving in the ninth century and pushed the Siboney and Guanahatabey to the western one-third of the island. The Arawak originated in South America and migrated northward along the West Indies archipelago. They had larger, permanent villages, usually numbering more than 1,000 inhabitants. The Arawak were also healthier and stronger than the Siboney and Guanahatabey because they grew most of their own food. Farming made their food supply dependable, abundant, and varied. They cooperated in planting, weeding, and harvesting their crops.

Christopher Columbus

Christopher Columbus first sighted Cuba during a driving rainstorm on the late afternoon of October 27, 1492. A few months earlier, the Spanish king had hired Columbus, an Italian adventurer and businessman, to find a sea route to India. This was his first voyage of discovery. Historians dispute exactly where he disembarked the next morning, but a location near Gibara, a small village on Cuba's northeast coast, is the most likely place.

Once on shore, the island's beauty astonished the explorer. Columbus wrote, "Everything I saw was so lovely that my eyes could not weary of beholding such beauty, nor could I weary of the songs of the birds large and small. . . . There are trees of a thousand species," he continued, "each has its particular fruit, and all of marvelous flavor." Columbus claimed this land for Spain. For the next five weeks, he sailed eastward along the indented northern coast, dropping anchor periodically in the many pouch-shaped harbors to explore the island.

Mindful that the Spanish Crown hired him to find the riches of India, he noted that Cuba's natives, whom he mistakenly called Indians because he thought they were inhabitants of India, wore what appeared to be silver jewelry. He also thought the island's pine forests would be a natural resource for shipbuilding. He was optimistic that there would be pearls in offshore waters, gold in streams, silver in the mountains, and spices in the mangrove forests. "It is certain that where there is such marvelous scenery, there must be much from which profit can be made," he noted. Columbus was convinced that he had found the riches of India.

Columbus's second voyage took him back to the West

Indies in November 1493. This time he sailed along Cuba's southern coast as far as the Gulf of Bataban. From there he sailed south to Cuba's second largest island, which he could see in the distance, and named it the Isle of Pines because of the large pine forest on the northern half of the island.

Motivated to find Cuba's riches, especially gold, Columbus explored the main island's southern coast for three months, before returning to Spain. He never discovered gold. He also never sailed around the west end of the island. If he had done so, he would have discovered that he had not found a continent. Instead, on this voyage he officially declared that Cuba was a peninsula of Asia. In 1503, the admiral made a third voyage to the West Indies, but only saw Cuba from a distance on his way back to Spain. In 1508, a Spaniard named Sebastián de Ocampo finally sailed around Cuba to prove that it was definitely an island.

Spanish Conquest and Colonial Period (1512-1898)

At first, Cuba did not receive much attention from Spain because it had only small deposits of gold. Occasionally, Spanish expeditions visited the island in search of able-bodied Indians to work as slaves in Hispaniola's gold mines and its newly established towns and plantations. The Arawaks fought back. However, their bows and arrows were no match against the raiders' mobility on horseback and their steel swords, muskets, and armor. The Spaniards overreacted to the Indian revolt and attacked swiftly and ruthlessly. They massacred tens of thousands of Indians. By 1519, the Indian population was down from its original size of 112,000 to just 19,000. By the end of the 16th century, it had shrunk to fewer than 2,000.

Diego de Velázquez, a wealthy landowner in western Hispaniola, led the conquest and early settlement of Cuba. The king of Spain made him the first governor of Cuba. Velázquez established the island's first seven Spanish settlements. He chose the sites of Baracoa (1512), Bayamo (1513), Trinidad (1514), Havana (1514), Puerto Príncipe (now Camagüey)

(1514), Sancti Spíritus (1514), and Santiago de Cuba (1515). Velázquez chose Santiago de Cuba as the island's first capital. Although this town was isolated at the eastern end of the island and surrounded by rugged mountains, it had a good harbor and was near the main trade routes at that time.

Cuba experienced an economic boost almost immediately after Velázquez's conquest. The Spanish Empire was expanding north into Florida, west into the Yucatán Peninsula and Mexico, and south into Venezuela, Columbia, and eventually Peru. Havana became the center of maritime activity. Job-seeking colonists from Spain were drawn to Cuba. Havana's large harbor, favorable currents and winds, and its location on the most direct route between Mexico, North America, and Europe made it the logical stopover point for expeditions to Spain's emerging empire.

Recognizing Havana's strategic importance, Spain built three fortresses around its harbor in the late 1500s to protect it from pirates and enemy warships. For the next two centuries, treasure fleets (flotas) from Vera Cruz in Mexico, Cartegena in Venezuela, and Panama City (known then as Puerto Bello) in Panama assembled there. From there, the fleets would take their cargos to Spain. A vast array of businesses developed around the needs of crews, passengers, and the city's growing population.

Havana became the colony's capital in 1607. By 1700, this port city accounted for more than half of the inhabitants on the island. Havana's population grew to 236,000 by 1899—a population more than five times greater than the second largest city, Santiago de Cuba, which had a population of only 43,100. The 1607 transfer of the political capital from Santiago de Cuba to Havana worsened conditions in eastern Cuba. Less official presence, including smaller army garrisons, made the eastern region more vulnerable to raids by pirates and enemy warships. Convoying Spain's treasure fleets through Havana isolated the former capital and reduced commerce there immensely. The eastern region's economy never flourished during the Spanish colonial period. However, its people survived and developed a strong distrust of Spain, Havana, and central control of government. Eastern Cuba is where future revolutionaries, such as José Martí and Fidel Castro, would first seek popular support from the people.

The Wars of Independence (1868-1898)

Cuba experienced two wars of independence during the second half of the 19th century. Both conflicts were responses to Spain's refusal to allow Cubans the right to govern themselves concerning local issues, such as taxation, public works, and trade policy. Cuban rebels in both conflicts used the impassioned political slogan, *Cuba Libre* (Free Cuba) as they fought against Spanish soldiers.

The First War of Independence (1868-1878) began on October 10, 1868, in eastern Cuba. The uprising failed in part because the rebels had weak leadership. The leaders who carried on the revolt, Máximo Gomez (a black man originally from the Dominican Republic) and Antonio Maceo (a former black slave), were inexperienced in conducting war and could not agree on strategy. Moreover, wealthy sugar plantation owners of western Cuba did not support the revolt. They feared that it would lead to the freeing of slaves, whom they depended on to work in their cane fields.

Seventeen years would pass between Cuba's First War of Independence and its second. The brilliant José Martí was the chief organizer, propagandist, fundraiser, and political leader of the Second War of Independence (1885-1898). He became Cuba's first national hero. Martí traveled to France, the United States, and Venezuela to raise financial support for an independent Cuba. He chose to start the war in eastern Cuba, where there was much popular sentiment for an uprising.

Martí enlisted key military leaders, including Gomez and Maceo (leaders of the First War of Independence), and returned to Cuba on April 11, 1885. After only a few weeks,

Spanish troops killed the 32-year-old Martí in a brief skirmish near the town of Dos Rios in today's Granma Province. However, Martí's vision and Gomez and Maceo's military experience routed the Spanish. (Nevertheless, Spaniards killed Maceo in a battle south of Havana before the war ended.)

Cubans shared their victory over Spain with American soldiers because the United States intervened and declared war against Spain on April 25, 1898. The Spanish-American War and the Second War of Independence ended shortly thereafter on August 2, 1898. Spain agreed to relinquish sovereignty over Cuba.

Spanish-American War and U.S. Occupation (1898-1902)

The Spanish-American War lasted less than four months. Cuban troops already had control over most of the island. On July 1, 1898, the U.S. Army attacked Spanish positions on San Juan Hill just east of Santiago de Cuba. The battle was bloody. Future President Theodore Roosevelt personally led the famous charge of the "Rough Riders" up San Juan Hill and claimed victory. Two days later, on July 3, the American navy destroyed the Spanish fleet when Spaniards tried to break out of the Bahía de Santiago de Cuba (Bay of Santiago).

Spain and the United States signed a peace treaty in Paris, thereby ending the Spanish-American War on December 12, 1898. The Cubans were not invited. The treaty included U.S. annexation of three Spanish colonies: Puerto Rico, Guam, and the Philippines. Only the Teller Amendment prevented the Americans from annexing Cuba. The United States placed Cuba under military occupation instead.

In November 1900, an assembly of elected Cuban delegates drew up a constitution similar to that of the United States. A year later, the U.S. Congress passed the Platt Amendment, giving the president the authority to send U.S. troops to Cuba whenever U.S. strategic interests and American lives there were threatened. The provisions of the amendment also enabled the United States to buy or lease land for naval bases in

Cuba. The United States gave Cuba the option of accepting the Platt Amendment or being under military occupation indefinitely. Cuba accepted the amendment.

Cuba became an independent republic on May 20, 1902, when its people elected Tomás Estrada Palma the first president of the Republic of Cuba. The United States withdrew its military forces from the island after the election.

The Republic (1902-1959)

A popular guidebook describes 1902 to 1959 in Cuba as the "Age of Decadence." During this period, the country had a series of presidents who led corrupt and incompetent governments. Moreover, during the years of the U.S. Prohibition (1919-1933), when alcohol was illegal in the United States, lavish Havana hotels, casinos, and brothels became a destination for American pleasure seekers. Additionally, members of organized crime in the United States rubbed shoulders with the Cuban elite at these establishments. Soon organized crime was operating Havana's casinos. American dollars tainted by corruption filled the pockets of many Cuban politicians. American corporations owned most of the farmland, essential services, and sugar mills.

The United States used the Platt Amendment to send troops to Cuba several times to put down labor strikes, riots, and armed rebellions—activities that jeopardized American business interests. The Platt Amendment kept corrupt governments in power at the expense of civil liberties aroused the collective indignation of the Cuban people. The American government ignored Cubans' angry protests. In 1903, under the provisions of the Platt Amendment, the United States obtained a permanent lease on Guantánamo Bay in southeastern Cuba and began construction of a naval base there. The United States still maintains the naval base, despite the hostility between the two countries today.

President Gerardo Machado (1924-1933) was one of Cuba's worst presidents. He relied on censorship, military force, and terror tactics in his last years, which coincided with a depression produced by the collapse of the world sugar market in 1930. Cuban discontent and U.S. pressure forced Machado to flee Cuba for the Bahamas in 1933.

Fulgencio Batista led a brief revolt to take power shortly after Machado fled. Batista ruled Cuba as army chief of staff or as president from 1933 to 1958. He got the United States to revoke the Platt Amendment in 1934 and instituted a liberal constitution in 1940. Nevertheless, Batista was an ineffective and corrupt leader. He hid bribery and extortion money in a bank account in Switzerland. He used a secret police force to root out, torture, and assassinate dissidents. He rigged elections and ignored the rural poverty, city slums, and crime that plagued the country.

On January 1, 1959, under pressure because of rebel victories in the countryside, Batista fled from Havana to the Dominican Republic and eventually to a comfortable exile in Spain. One week after the infamous Batista left Havana, the charismatic Fidel Castro, leader of Cuba's rebel army, entered the city a national hero.

The Cuban Revolution (1953-1959)

Castro's plan for a Cuban revolution started poorly. On July 26, 1953, he led a band of 119 rebels in an unsuccessful attack on the Moncada army barracks in Santiago de Cuba, the most important military base in eastern Cuba at the time. Government troops captured Castro. He stayed in prison until Batista granted a general amnesty in 1955.

Upon his release from prison, Castro organized a small group of underground leaders in eastern Cuba. It would be the underground's job to recruit members of the local population for a popular uprising. Castro moved to Mexico and used money from Cuban exiles in the United States to organize and train a small military force of 82 men. He called the force M (Movement)-26-7, after the date of the failed July 26 attack on the Moncada barracks.

Fulgencio Batista came to power through dishonest elections and played a role in the army or government for 25 years. Even though he stressed the development of industry and invited foreign companies to open in Cuba, the people remained poor and there was much unrest.

Castro and the M-26-7 force returned to Cuba on December 2, 1956, in a leaky yacht named the *Granma*. They landed at Cape Cruz in eastern Cuba. Batista's army crushed the rebel force shortly after it landed. Castro and 11 others (including future commanders and revolutionary heroes Ernesto "Che" Guevara, Fidel's brother Raúl, and Camilo Cienfuegos) managed to escape into the Sierra Maestra range.

At first, Castro's underground was unable to rally the local population to his cause. However, by the end of 1957, Castro's revolution had captured the imagination of the Cuban people. Castro's army had grown in size. His rebels were making guerrilla warfare, descending from the mountains to raid cane plantations and mines, and then hiding out in the mountains again. A radio station, set up at his headquarters in the Sierra Maestra, kept the people informed of the revolution's growing strength.

Graham Greene, author of *Our Man in Havana*, was traveling in Cuba at the time. He wrote, "The Oriente Province [eastern Cuba] almost to the last man, woman and child was on the side of Fidel." Castro had repulsed efforts by Batista's army to push him from his Sierra Maestra stronghold. Raúl Castro controlled a second eastern front in the Sierra de Cristal. Together, the Castro brothers had Santiago de Cuba (Cuba's second largest city) surrounded. Guevara and Cienfuegos were in charge of a third force in the Sierra del Escambray of central Cuba. By mid-1958, all three forces could hold their own in pitched battles against government troops.

In late November 1958, Castro's forces moved quickly out of the mountains. They scored major victories against Bastista's army in large cities: Santiago de Cuba, Bayamo, and Santa Clara. In December, the armies of Guevara and Ceinfuegos had victories in central Cuba and then swiftly moved toward Havana, compelling Batista to flee the country. The cause of Cuba Libre seemed to have finally cast out the last dictator and foreign power from Cuban soil.

Castro Moves Toward Communism (1959-1961)

When Castro took power, he was not a Communist. However, a series of events—involving the Soviet Union, Cuba, and the United States—moved him toward Communism and into the Cold War.

Shortly after taking power, Castro made it clear that he was not going to create a government based on coalitions with Cuba's wealthy elite, many whom had close ties with the United

States. He held "war crimes" trials that targeted wealthy Cubans and the political opposition in 1959. As the news cameras rolled, Castro cold-heartedly condemned prisoners to death. Castro and Castro-appointed judges threw countless other opposition members into prison or exiled them. Firing squads executed more than 600 people after these mock trials. Castro had the trials televised live. Hundreds of thousands of Cuban political refugees poured into the United States. Castro's ruthless treatment of the political opposition greatly disturbed and alienated freedom-loving people throughout the world.

Nor was Castro going to return Cuba to foreign domination. As part of his agrarian reform, he seized landholdings of large U.S. companies such as the United Fruit Company. In the summer of 1960 he seized U.S. and British oil companies for their refusal to refine Soviet petroleum. In August 1960 the Cuban government seized the American-owned telephone and electricity companies and sugar mills. Castro believed correctly that the U.S. Central Intelligence Agency (CIA) was hatching plots against him in the U.S. embassy in Havana. He told the United States to reduce its embassy staff from 300 to 11 persons.

President Dwight D. Eisenhower responded to Castro's actions in January 1961 by breaking off official diplomatic relations with Cuba, imposing a trade embargo, and banning U.S. citizens from traveling there. The U.S. policy since then has been to isolate Cuba geographically and diplomatically.

The Bay of Pigs Invasion

The Bay of Pigs invasion dashed any hope that Cuba might stop its slide toward Communism. The invasion took place on April 14, 1961. It involved about 1,400 anti-Castro Cuban refugees. President Kennedy permitted the U.S. Navy to escort the invaders' ships to Cuban waters but canceled use of U.S. planes by anti-Castro pilots in the actual fighting.

The battle took place where the invaders disembarked, at the Bay of Pigs, just west of Cienfuegos. The fighting lasted three days.

Castro's troops and local militias killed more than 100 invaders and took the survivors prisoner. The defeat of the invaders made Castro a national hero for a second time. Castro declared that Cuba should become a communist-style state on April 16, 1961— during the Bay of Pigs invasion. In a speech in December 1961, he declared that he was a true believer in Communism.

The Cuban Missile Crisis

Tensions between Cuba and the United States peaked during the 1962 Cuban Missile Crisis. That event, which involved high stakes diplomacy between President Kennedy and Nikita Khrushchev (the Soviet Union's premier), brought the world close to the brink of nuclear war.

The crisis began when U.S. high altitude reconnaissance aircraft spotted Soviet Union nuclear missiles inside Cuba that were capable of striking anywhere in the United States. The crisis ended when Khrushchev agreed to dismantle and remove the missiles after receiving secret assurance from Kennedy that the United States would not invade Cuba. The United States also promised to withdraw some of its nuclear missiles from Turkey (which borders the former Soviet Union).

Afterward, Castro and the Americans continued to engage in a war of hostile diplomacy. Relations between the United States and Cuba deteriorated rapidly, and the Castro regime moved toward adopting a one-party Communist system. The Soviet Union encouraged this move by giving Cuba loans and military aid. The Soviet Union also became the island's main supplier of food and fuel. The Soviets also agreed to buy any sugar the United States refused to purchase. The Soviet Union became Cuba's main trading partner.

Cuba–U.S. Relations (1965-2002)

Cuba officially became a Communist government in 1965. The country started receiving military aid from the Soviet Union and Eastern European Communist countries. Castro used this aid

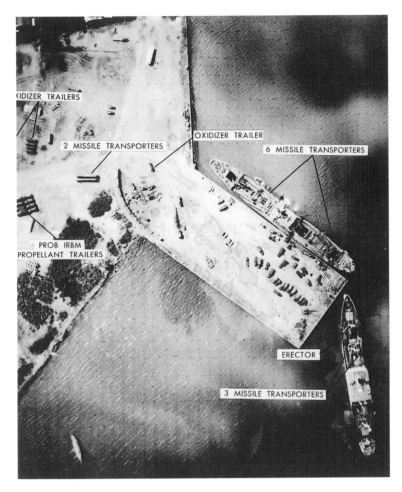

KIDIZER TRAILERS

OXIDIZER TRAILER

2 MISSILE TRANSPORTERS

6 MISSILE TRANSPORTERS

PROB IRBM
PROPELLANT TRAILERS

ERECTOR

3 MISSILE TRANSPORTERS

The Cuban Missile Crisis occurred in October 1962 when the United States identified evidence that the Soviet Union had built a nuclear missile launching base in Cuba. The missiles were positioned to be able to hit targets in the United States.

to support guerrilla movements (*focos*) in Africa and several countries in Latin America. Castro even sent Cuban troops to fight in some of these countries. Bolivian troops killed Che Guevara, one of Castro's most trusted commanders during the Cuban revolution, and 38 of his men, while attempting to start such a movement in Bolivia. The United States protested vigorously against Cuba's policy of exporting revolution.

Elián Gonzáles, shown here with Fidel Castro, was the subject of a custody battle between his father in Cuba and relatives in Florida. The boy had been rescued after his mother died while trying to flee Cuba by crossing the Straits of Florida in a boat.

remaining portion of Cuba's 1959-1960 sugar imports and by banning U.S. exports to Cuba, except certain foodstuffs and medical supplies. Kennedy imposed the total ban on trade 1961. Additionally, the U.S. government froze all Cuban-owned assets in the United States and forbade American tourists from traveling to Cuba.

In 1992 the U.S. government passed the Cuba Democracy Act. The act has two tracks. The first track discourages trade with Cuba by preventing foreign businesses owned by U.S. companies from trading with the island and by preventing foreign vessels that are carrying Cuban goods from entering U.S. ports. The second track allows Cuban Americans to visit their relatives in Cuba once a year. This track allows personal contacts, but does not directly benefit the Castro government.

The U.S. Helms-Burton Act of 1996 is the most recent economic sanction taken by the United States against Cuba. It was a U.S. response to the 1996 downing of the Brothers to the Rescue aircraft over international waters. This act authorizes the U.S. president to prevent business executives of foreign countries from entering the United States if their companies use U.S. property seized by the Castro government. The law also gives American businesses the right to sue in U.S. court any foreign nations that benefit or profit from using the seized property.

Although the Helms-Burton law is well intentioned, U.S. presidents have been reluctant to use it. The law would require that the United States take action against allies and important trading partners of the United States. These partners include Canada, Mexico, the United Kingdom, Germany, Russia, and France. All of these countries conduct trade with Cuba today.

Cautious engagement between Cuba and the United States is taking place now. The United States modified its trade sanctions laws in 2000 to allow trade with Cuba in agricultural commodities, medicines, and medical supplies. However, the purchaser cannot be controlled, owned, or operated by the Cuban government. Until recently, the government controlled, owned, and operated all means of production in the country. In mid-December 2001 the first American ship to dock in Cuba in almost 40 years arrived in Havana with a shipment of food and medicine from the United States.

Children light candles as part of a Santería mass. This popular Afro-Cuban form of religion is widely practiced in Cuba and combines African beliefs with some Christian ceremonies.

4

People and Culture

Population Distribution

C uba has the largest population among Caribbean countries. The island has 11.2 million inhabitants. (The Dominican Republic is second largest with about 5.6 million people.) Due to its large land area, Cuba has the lowest population density in the region, with 262 persons per square mile (101 persons per square kilometer). The island's population is highly urbanized, with 70 percent of the people living in cities. The country's low population density and concentration of people in cities means that rural areas are sparsely settled.

Like two poles of a magnet, Cuba's population is concentrated on opposite ends of the island (Table 1). Thirty-nine percent of the population resides in the western provinces and mainly in the major urban areas of Havana, Matanzas, and Pinar del Río. Another

36 percent of the population is in the eastern provinces and mostly in the cities of Santiago de Cuba, Las Tunas, Bayamo, Holguín, and Guantánamo. The remaining 25 percent of the population resides in the central provinces, which include the cities of Santa Clara, Sancti Spirítus, Cienfuegos, Santa Clara, Ciego de Avila, and Camagüey.

Table 1: Provinces and Their Populations (1990)

REGION	PROVINCE	POPULATION
West	Havana City	2,106,600
	Havana	647,3000
	Matanzas	612,300
	Pinar del Río	694,300
Central	Camagüey	744,700
	Ciego de Avila	367,500
	Cienfuegos	366,500
	Sancti Spíritus	430,700
	Villa Clara	810,200
East	Granma	739,900
	Guantánamo	499,200
	Holguín	997,700
	Las Tunas	495,100
	Santiago de Cuba	995,400
*Special municipality	Isla de la Juventud	73,300

*The Isla de la Juventud is not part of any province. Its affairs are overseen directly by the central government.

Population Growth Slows Down

When the Cuban Revolution ended in 1959, the island's population was 6.9 million. Since Fidel Castro took over the government Cuba's population has continued to grow, but in decreasing numbers (Table 2). Cuba now has one of the lowest population growth rates in Latin America (0.37 percent in 2001).

The large number of dissatisfied Cubans leaving Castro's Cuba each year slowed the rate of population increase. As mentioned in Chapter 3, hundreds of thousands of boat people have left the island illegally since 1980. Moreover, since 1994, the Castro government has allowed 20,000 Cubans to emigrate legally each year. The government uses a lottery to determine who may leave the country. An estimated 500,000 Cubans have signed up to be included in the lottery.

Table 2: Cuba's Slowdown in Population Increase by Decade 1961-2000

DECADE	POPULATION INCREASE
1961-1970	1,435,100
1971-1980	1,032,000
1981-1990	874,000
1991-2000	448,000

Nevertheless, thousands of additional Cubans emigrate illegally annually. The U.S. Central Intelligence Agency estimates that 3,000 Cubans came over water on the Straits of Florida in 2000. The U.S. Coast Guard stopped about one-third of these migrants. In the same year, another 2,400 Cubans arrived overland illegally. These people either slipped across the U.S.-Mexico border, or took direct flights to Miami from various Latin American cities. Because so many dissatisfied people have emigrated from Cuba since 1959, more than half of the country's population is under the age of 40.

Other factors besides emigration contribute to Cuba's slow population growth, including higher education levels, better health care, birth control, and greater female participation in the work force. Additionally, Cuba's loss of trade with the former Soviet Union beginning in 1991 created a severe shortage of money, consumer goods, and housing. Consequently, married couples cannot afford to have as many children.

Population Composition

The Cuban population is composed of mulattos (of black-Spanish descent), 51 percent; whites (*criollos*), 37 percent; blacks (Afro-Cubans), 11 percent; and Chinese, 1 percent. There is little trace of the Indian population today, except for archaeological sites. Unlike most former Spanish colonies, there are almost no people of Indian-Spanish descent. War, hard labor, disease, and suicide almost wiped out Cuba's native Indians very quickly.

Before the revolution, it was typical for whites to discriminate against blacks both socially and in employment. One of the first acts of the Castro government was to make racial discrimination illegal. Cuban society now accepts mixed marriages as commonplace. The proportion of blacks and mulattos is increasing gradually due to improvements in health services and because most Cubans leaving the country are white. Almost all Cuban whites are of Spanish origin.

Some white families came to Cuba from Spain in the early colonial period. Other criollos are descendants of Spaniards that arrived from other Spanish colonies that gained independence from Spain in the early 1800s. Still other whites are descended from immigrants that came to Cuba from Spain and the Canary Islands (a Spanish colony in the Atlantic Ocean) between 1900 and 1933. About 750,000 Spaniards arrived during that period. Although the number of later immigrants was smaller, Cuba remained a favorite destination of people from Spain until the revolution.

Many blacks in Cuba are descendants of African slaves. The Spaniards imported African slaves to replace the Indians as laborers. Slave traders brought 800,000 West African blacks shackled in irons. Most black slaves belonged to the Yoruba and

Bantu tribes, and some of their original traditions survive today in various Afro-Cuban religions.

During the colonial period, the number of "free colored" people in Cuba was greater than in other Caribbean societies. Around 1800, the geographer Alexander von Humboldt visited Cuba and observed, "In no part of the world, where slavery prevails is emancipation [freeing of slaves] so frequent as in the island of Cuba." The large proportion of free blacks rose from Cuba's legal system. It allowed slave owners to free their slaves, if the slaves would agree to pay for their freedom. Many slave owners often found this practice profitable. In the mid-1800s, the conversion of sugar mills from manual power to steam power reduced the demand for slave labor. This change in technology also enabled more blacks to purchase their freedom and to enter the general Cuban population.

In 1886, Spain ended all forms of slavery in Cuba. Blacks, both slave and free, made up one-third of the total population, or about 500,000 of 1.5 million people. The proportion of blacks has decreased since then. An exception to the black population's downward trend took place between 1919 and 1926, when plantation owners in Cuba recruited 250,000 black laborers from Jamaica and Haiti to work for wages on sugarcane plantations.

There was some infusion of French culture into Cuba's white and black populations in the early 1800s. Several thousand French-speaking whites and African black slaves came to eastern Cuba from Haiti (a French colony) at that time. These emigrants were seeking safety from Haiti's war of independence from France. French cultural influence is still apparent in the cities of eastern Cuba, the main destination of people fleeing the conflict. Additional French immigrants came from the Louisiana Territory following purchase of the territory from France in 1803. Many of these emigrants settled in what is now Cienfuegos Province.

The Chinese element is very small. Cuban plantation

operators imported 125,000 Chinese laborers into Cuba between 1847 and 1874. The Chinese came from southern China, which was experiencing a tremendous surge in population. (During this same period, Chinese emigrant laborers were also mining gold in California and building railroads in the United States.)

The Chinese came to Cuba as indentured servants, which meant that they signed contracts promising to work for a minimum number of years. (Their contracts were for a minimum of eight years.) No women were in this population; Cuba was in need of male laborers that could do back-breaking work in sugarcane fields and construction projects. Unfortunately, the plantation bosses treated these early immigrants like slaves. The bosses often shackled them in irons, and they were menaced with whips by the guards assigned to watch them. Plantation owners brought another 30,000 southern Chinese laborers to the island in the 1920s. The bosses treated this later group more humanely.

Few Chinese could afford to pay for a ship's passage back to China after their contracts ended. Many who stayed married black Cuban women. A small Chinatown in Havana is a reminder of this part of Cuba's cultural history. Additionally, rice—an important staple to the Chinese diet—became a fixture in the Cuban diet as well.

Race Relations

Before the Cuban Revolution, skin color was a divisive issue. Blacks, especially, had little access to good jobs. Racial prejudice blocked them from joining white country clubs and attending white private schools. Cuban whites were insensitive to the feelings of people of color; they often used terms such as *El Chino* (the Chinese man), *El Negrito* (the black one), and *La Mulata* (the mulatto one).

Today, making racial distinctions is a social taboo. People of all races receive the same care in hospitals and attend the same schools. Intermarriage between whites and blacks is commonplace, and virtually all neighborhoods are integrated. Nevertheless, there is evidence that racial discrimination persists. There is no black political leader of significant power. The proportion of black Cubans earning university degrees is low compared to that of white Cubans. Additionally, there are noticeably more whites occupying lucrative jobs as waitresses, doormen, tour guides, and cab drivers in the tourism industry. Even Castro has acknowledged in recent years that there are "lingering traces of racial discrimination in Cuba."

Language

Spanish is the official language of Cuba. Knowledge of it is necessary for a visitor traveling around the country. Almost all newspapers, magazines, books, signs, documents, maps, menus, and museum captions are in Spanish only.

Cubans use some words of Indian, African, and English origin. They use Indian nouns to identify many mountains, rivers, and towns. For example, the name "Cuba" comes from the word *cubanacán*, meaning a center or central place. *Ceiba*, is the Indian name for a prominent tree on the island. *Sabana* is the Indian name for grassland. Camagüey, the main city in central Cuba is also of Indian origin. Hurricane is another Indian term, meaning *big wind* in the Arawak (Taíno) language.

African terms include names of various plants and animals, such as *afi*, a species of yucca. *Mambí*, the African name for rebel fighters, is the name given to pro-Castro guerrilla fighters during the Cuban Revolution. Many words of African origin—such as rumba, mambo, and conga—deal with aspects of African religion and music found in Cuba.

Cubans do not speak much English. Primary schools only teach it in sixth grade. Therefore, ordinary people speak only some English and then very poorly. Nevertheless, Cuba's proximity to the United States has a strong influence on everyday speech. Many English words concern baseball, boxing, automobiles, and popular brand names of American products. An example of English word usage involving boxing is as follows: "*Mohammed Ali le solt dos uppercuts y trés jabs que lo dejaron groggy*" (Mohammed Ali threw out two uppercuts and three jabs that left him [the opponent] groggy).

Before Castro took over the government, more Cubans spoke English, as the educated middle and upper classes had dealings with American businessmen and tourists. Castro's policy of confiscating the property and bank accounts of Cuban "capitalists" forced most of these English-speakers to flee Cuba. In recent years, there has been a growing interest in learning English again. A good command of English is a key to jobs in the tourist industry, which is a way to potentially access U.S. dollars.

Religion

Most outsiders think of Cuba as a Catholic country because it is a former Spanish colony. Before Castro took power, however, Cuba was the least religious country in Latin America. Only about 10 percent of the population regularly attended church. Nevertheless, the Castro government tries to discourage religion. Communist governments view any form of organized religion as a threat. Communism requires allegiance of the individual to the State. The Christian religion asks for allegiance to God. Moreover, Communist governments view the Christian religion with great suspicion because it has a hierarchy of worshipers, priests, bishops, archbishops, cardinals, and a pope. Communist governments view this hierarchy as a possible network for antigovernment conspiracies.

The Castro government pressured into exile about 90 percent of the practicing Catholics and Catholic priests in the country by 1965. The government did not necessarily target Catholics for their religious beliefs, as the wealthy and middle class Cubans leaving the country for political reasons made up most of the practicing Catholic population. Nevertheless, the

Cuban government continues to stifle organized religion by banning the distribution of religious literature and the airing of religious television and radio programs.

Castro eased up on suppression of religion by allowing Pope John Paul II to visit Cuba in January 1998. The Pope celebrated open-air masses in Havana, Santa Clara, Camagüey, and Santiago de Cuba. The government gave the Catholic Council of Churches permission to distribute 100,000 bibles as gifts during the papal visit. Cuban experts see the pope's visit as a hopeful sign that the Castro government is feeling less threatened by religion than it did before.

The most widespread form of religion in Cuba today is neither Protestant nor Catholic, but a belief system called Santería—"way of the saints." This system teaches that Afro-Cuban gods and spirits (*orishas*) inhabit forests. Therefore, forests are sacred. Santería is the largest of the Afro-Cuban religions. African Yoruba slaves (from a region that is now in Nigeria) developed the religion as a way to trick slave owners: while publicly professing their worship of Catholic saints, the slaves privately venerated animistic gods and goddesses of their homeland. Believers worship these African spirits through plant, food, and animal sacrifices offered during chants and dancing initiations. Cubans in Havana do not call this religion Santería; they prefer to call it the "Yoruba religion" after its place of origin.

Some Catholic priests welcome Santería as a way to attract parishioners to Christian teachings, while others see it as evil. Many worshipers regard themselves as Roman Catholics. They believe that the names of the Catholic saints are Spanish translations of Yoruban names of orishas. There are more Santería priests in Havana than Catholic priests in all of Cuba.

There are two smaller African religions in Cuba. African Bantus brought the first, Regla Cona, to Cuba. It originated in the Congo region of Africa. African slaves from Nigeria brought the second, Abakuá. Worshipers practice Abakuá mainly in the provinces of Havana and Matanzas.

African religions swear their worshipers to secrecy, a tradition that slaves developed to avoid punishment from their white masters for practicing a non-Catholic religion. Although African slaves were responsible for the emergence of these religions, they have gained in popularity among every race on the island. The priests of Afro-Cuban religions have no hierarchy or centralized leadership. Therefore, they have never been a threat to the Castro government. Freedom from persecution may explain why such religions are so popular.

Cuban Music and Dance

Cuban music and dance reveal the soul of Cuban culture: They bring together Cuba's African and European traditions, offering a distinct blend of the two. Fernando Ortiz, a Cuban social historian, described Cuban music as "a love affair between the African drum and the Spanish guitar." The Cuban-American scholar William Luis says in *Culture and Customs of Cuba,* "Cuban music is lively, energetic, and invigorating, but also soft sensual, and emotional. The music makes listeners want to dance and touches the deepest parts of the soul. Indeed, Cubans carry music in their blood."

Cuban music and dance are inseparable. They are the most famous expressions of Cuban culture. The Cuban *son,* an Afro-Cuban music form, came first. A combination of Cuban dance and music called the rumba came next. Cuban and North American musicians made the son and rumba and their variants famous in the 20th century by modifying them into popular forms of entertainment.

Son was the first music to successfully mix Spanish lyrics with African rhythm. The son originated in the mountains of eastern Cuba and became popular in the cities there in the late 19th century. The radio popularized it throughout Cuba in the 1920s. In its original form, groups performing son music used guitars, bongos (a pair of small round drums joined by a piece of

Music and dance are important parts of Cuban culture. The rhythms and words bring together various elements form Cuba's different ethnic groups.

wood), a base, claves (two wooden sticks tapped together to set the beat), and maracas (gourd-shaped rattles). The son involved music, not dancing. A variation of the son is the rumba, which gave rise to several other forms of music and dance.

The rumba is an Afro-Cuban music and dance combination that began in the early 20th century in urban centers and small settlements around sugarcane mills. Like the son, the rumba combines Spanish lyrics and African rhythm, but the African rhythm is stronger. The rumba features a soloist and chorus and a single dancer or pair of dancers. The musical instruments include a clave, the drum, the *quinto* (a higher-pitched drum), and spoons.

The rumba spread to New York in the 1920s where orchestras changed it into a big band ballroom dance with the addition of horns and strings. The rumba is rich and has many variants, including combination music and dance forms called the conga, mambo, and the cha-cha.

Conga music is a variation of the rumba. It is possibly of Bantu origin and includes the conga drum. The conga drum is a tall barrel-like drum held together by metal hoops. Musicians and participants dance in a line, improvising steps.

The mambo has a fast beat and uses the violin, flute, piano, contrabass, timbale, and guiro (an elongated gourd rasped with a stick, although there are tin guiros). Later it acquired a conga drum, two violins, and three singers. A Cuban musician invented a ballroom dance, the cha-cha, in the late 1940s to appeal to North American dancers. The cha-cha is not too fast, it is easy to learn, and it has simple lyrics to the songs.

Cuban music has been popular in the United States. RCA Victor and Columbia Records launched their record companies in the 1940s by featuring Cuban musicians. Well-known Cuban musicians, such as Xavier Cugat, who composed music and appeared in many Hollywood movies, promoted Cuban music. Desi Arnaz, a Cuban, married comedian Lucille Ball and was featured on the *I Love Lucy* show. He popularized the conga line in the United States.

Authentic Cuban music and dance have declined in popularity since about 1980. A loosely defined style related to jazz, called salsa, has replaced them. East Coast musicians in the United States developed salsa. It is a mixture of the Cuban son and other Latin rhythms.

Cuban Sports

If Cuban music and dance reveal the soul of Cuban culture, then Cuban baseball reveals its heart. As in the United States, baseball is Cuba's national pastime. The adoption of a team sport as a national pastime is important to a country, as its popularity cuts across lines of class, age, race, gender, and politics; it appeals to people living in cities and in rural areas. It teaches people of diverse backgrounds that they can work together toward a common goal.

Cuba is the first country outside of the United States to play

Cubans are enthusiastic baseball fans and players, sometimes even taking on a team from the United States. The Baltimore Orioles were in Havana in 1999 to play against the Cuban All Stars.

baseball. Cubans built the first baseball stadium in Matanzas in 1874. After the Spanish-American War, U.S. soldiers stationed on the island played against the islanders. Cubans have had a passion for baseball ever since.

Baseball has brought greater contact between Cuban and U.S. cultures. Games between the Baltimore Orioles and Cuban All Stars have been a regular event for several years. Additionally, more than a few Cubans have played in the major leagues, including the well-known Pedro (Tony) Oliva. He played for the Minnesota Twins, was named the American League Rookie of the Year in 1964, and won three batting titles in his career. Mike Cuellar, who first played for the Havana

Sugar Kings, won the Cy Young Award playing for the Baltimore Orioles in 1969, the only Cuban to do so. Tony Pérez played for a sugar factory in Cuba and signed with the Cincinnati Reds in 1960. Seven years later he became the Red's most valuable player (MVP). Pérez became a member of the Baseball Hall of Fame in 1970.

There were many other Cuban players with outstanding records in American baseball: Sandy Amars, Orestes (Minnie) Miñoso, Camillo Pasual, Tony Taylor, Octavio (Cookie) Rojas, Pedro Dagoberto Blanco (Tony) Campaneris, and Luis Tiant Jr. Other famous American players were born in Cuba, but they did not play in Cuba. For example, José Canseco (Oakland Athletics and Florida Marlins) and Rafael Palmeiro (Baltimore Orioles) were born in Havana, but they came to the United States when they were youngsters.

Cuban baseball has had to make adjustments under Castro. Entrance fees to games are much lower now, so that less money is available to pay for equipment. As a result, Cuban teams must use aluminum bats because they break less often than the expensive wooden bats. Fans must return foul balls because they are too expensive to replace. Additionally, night games are no longer possible due to the country's fuel shortage.

More serious is the defection of the island's star players. For example, Iván Hernández joined the Florida Marlins in 1996 and became the MVP of the World Series in 1997. The next year, his half-brother, Orlando "El Duque" Hernández, defected. El Duque signed a contract with the New York Yankees where he made important contributions to the team's victories in the 1998 and 1999 World Series.

Boxing, in addition to baseball, has had a long-standing tradition in Cuba. Additionally, Cubans are outstanding competitors in track and field, judo, volleyball, water polo, and weightlifting. The Castro government is largely responsible for Cuba's reputation as a world leader in sports. It established a sports academy system where promising athletes continue their education while they receive specialized training in sports.

American Cultural Influences

Louis A. Pérez, a Cuban-American and author of *On Being Cuban: Identity, Nationality, and Culture,* describes how Cubans developed a uniquely Cuban culture. They did this, Pérez says, by adopting certain aspects of American culture and rejecting aspects of Spanish culture. He summarizes the American influence on Cuba's culture during the first half of the 20th century in this passage:

> Cuba was a country in which many citizens knew something about big-league [American] baseball and professional boxing. Cubans participated eagerly in North American consumer culture and developed loyalties to U.S. brand names. They were unabashedly devoted to Hollywood, its movies and movie stars. In remote country stores it was common for rural consumers to have direct access to canned foods and ready-made clothing, as well as tools and farm equipment, manufactured in the United States, not as instruments of oppression, but as material goods eagerly adopted to improve daily life.

The influence of American culture on Cubans continues today. Mass media, as well as Spanish television and radio broadcasts from stations in Florida, reinforce this influence every day. Additionally, American merchandise purchased on the black market, such as videos and reading materials, influences Cubans' preferences and attitudes.

The Capitolio Nacional is located just outside of Old Havana. The building was constructed in 1929 to serve as the seat of the legislature. The Academy of Sciences and the Natural History Museum now occupy it.

5

Government

Cuba's Provinces

The population of colonial Cuba spread very slowly. Consequently, Spain did not create political units on the island until 1827. In that year, the Spanish began to govern the island through three loosely defined departments: Occidental (Western), Central (Central), and Oriente (Eastern). The departments were under the command of a captain general, who lived in Havana. Each department had several towns. The towns had broad areas of sparsely settled land separating them. Mayors and judges within each department collected taxes and administered the law. To the chagrin of the colonists, the king appointed officials who were only of pure Spanish descent.

The provinces of Cuba today have their origins in 1879. By then, colonists had established many new settlements, particularly in the interior of the island. The bloody First War of Independence had just ended. The captain general had to control Cuba's still rebellious population. He wanted to occupy the island with his troops in clearly defined areas. The six provinces that he established were Pinar del Río, Havana, Matanzas, Las Villas, Camagüey, and Oriente.

Cuba's population was about 1.5 million in 1879. It grew fourfold to 6 million by 1959. Yet, the same six provinces still made up the country. The government finally revised its constitution in 1976 to include the island's current 14 provinces.

Table 3 summarizes the changes in Cuba's provincial boundaries in 1976. The government made the fewest changes in western Cuba. The boundaries of two western provinces, Pinar del Río and Matanzas, had hardly changed at all. However, the city of Havana's population (1.75 million) was so large that it became a separate province. The rest of Havana province remained in tact. In central Cuba, Las Villas became three provinces—Cienfuegos, Sancti Spíritus, and Villa Clara.

Table 3: Origin of Cuba's Provinces

1827 TO 1879 DEPARTMENTS	1879 TO 1976 PROVINCES	1976 TO PRESENT PROVINCES
West	Havana	Havana
	Havana	Havana City
	Matanzas	Matanzas
	Pinar del Río	Pinar del Río
Central	Camagüey	Camagüey
		Ciego de Avila
	Las Villas	Cienfuegos
		Sancti Spíritus
		Villa Clara
East	Oriente	Granma
		Guantánamo
		Holguín
		Las Tunas
		Santiago de Cuba

Additionally, the former Camagüey Province became two provinces—Ciego de Avila and Camagüey. Finally, the division of Oriente Province yielded five provinces—Granma, Guantánamo, Holguín, Las Tunas, and Santiago de Cuba.

Republic of Cuba (1902-1959)

In 1902, Cuba created a republican government similar to that of the United States. It had three branches. The executive branch consisted of a president and a cabinet appointed by the president. The legislative branch was bicameral (a two-house body) consisting of a Senate and House. Voters elected 54 senators, 9 from each of the country's six provinces. The number of house members that voters elected from each province depended on the population size of the province. The larger the province the greater the number of house members.

The judicial branch included a Supreme Court that interpreted laws and made rulings on court cases appealed to it by lower courts. There were six District Courts; each had a province in its jurisdiction (territorial range of authority). District Courts ruled on cases dealing with provincial matters and they oversaw lower courts that had jurisdictions at the municipal level.

A republican government allows its citizens to form political parties and to elect people to represent them. Cuba's republican period had serious political turmoil, which led to labor strikes, demonstrations, and riots. Opposing political parties even resorted to terror tactics, such as kidnappings and bombings. The Cuban military took over the government several times. Additionally, the United States used the Platt Amendment to bring in U.S. troops on several occasions. The Cubans were unable to function as an independent republic. This left doors open for the 1959 Cuban Revolution and Communism.

Communist Government (1959-Present)

Cuba's government has been a one-party Communist government since 1965. All other political parties are illegal.

The government divided provinces into municipalities for voting purposes. (Municipalities are similar to counties in the United States.) Voters in each municipality elect Communist Party members to municipal assemblies. The assemblies choose members of the National Assembly, the government's legislative branch. Members of the National Assembly have five-year terms. Municipality voters also elect members to provincial governments. Since there are no other political parties, voters can only elect Communist Party members to office.

Communism seeks to abolish capitalism, which is an economic system based on individual ownership and enterprise in a free market economy. Supply and demand drive the prices of goods and services in such an economy. In contrast, a Communist state emphasizes the requirements of the state, rather than individual liberties. People do not even own their own homes. The state owns all homes and operates all farms, factories, schools, businesses, railroads, television stations, newspapers, sports teams and facilities, banks, apartments, and so on. The state sets the prices of most goods. The state also tries to distribute wealth evenly by setting similar wages for jobs that require very different skills. Hence, a factory worker might earn as much money as a medical doctor.

Communism is disappearing from the community of nations. It has serious economic and political shortcomings. The state's leveling of wages and controlling of prices discourages people from working hard. This low productivity results in poor quality and scarcity of goods. People seek more and better products; smuggling, bribery, theft, and other crimes become problems. Additionally, Communism's one-party system does not allow citizens to organize a political opposition in order to change the government peacefully.

Cuba is one of the few remaining Communist countries in the world. It does not remain communist because of any inherent economic or political virtues. It remains Communist largely because of Fidel Castro and a group of his closest

Fidel Castro is the leader of the country and the president of the National Assembly. He has ruled as a dictator over his Communist country since 1959.

advisers. Through Castro's leadership, the Communist Party and a secret police force suppress any political dissent that might lead to the replacement of Communism.

Government Structure

Fidel Castro is a dictator: he controls all major social, economic, and political activities in the country. He is first secretary of the Communist Party, chief of state, head of government, and commander in chief of the armed forces. Castro shares power only with his brother, Raúl, and with a few other associates. Raúl Castro serves as first vice president of the Council of State and first vice president of the Council of Ministers as well as minister of defense.

The Cuban legislature is a unicameral (one-house body) called the National Assembly. The National Assembly is, in fact, the Communist Party's elected representative body. Communist Party members in hundreds of Cuban municipalities elect members to the 601-member assembly. Members serve five-year terms. The next election is in 2003. The National Assembly meets only twice a year for a few days each time. It elects the president and vice president. In the last election (1998), the assembly elected Fidel Castro as president by a 100 percent vote and his brother Raúl as vice president by a 100 percent vote. The next election for these offices is not scheduled.

The National Assembly essentially rubber-stamps political appointments. It also passes legislation that Fidel Castro desires. When the assembly is not meeting, the Council of State, which has 31 members, governs the country. As its president, Castro has final say on all political matters before the council.

The Council of Ministers is the executive branch of government. It has 37 members that are controlled by Castro. This body is comparable to the U.S. governments' cabinet. Each minister oversees a particular government function (e.g., the minister of transportation oversees the building and maintenance of roads.). Castro has the power to dismiss ministers from office. He can even redefine the function of a ministry. One ministry, the Ministry of the Interior, is Castro's main government office for gathering intelligence. The information is used to crackdown on political dissidents. Loyal members of the Communist Party, who report on suspicious activities, behavior, or conversations, supply most of the intelligence.

The constitution provides for independent courts. Nevertheless, Castro controls them as the head of the National Assembly and the Council of State. The People's Supreme Court is the highest judicial body. The courts, from the People's Supreme Court down, routinely deny due process (the right to a fair and speedy trial) to political protesters. The courts' denial of due process in political cases is legal. The Cuban constitution states that judges can deny all legally recognized civil liberties to anyone that opposes the "decision of the Cuban people to build socialism."

The Communist Party decides who gets government jobs and promotions, including judgeships. Party membership is a prerequisite for high-level government positions. The party promotes its members in professions (such as education, medicine, and law) before they do nonmembers.

Revolutionary Armed Forces

Cuba became a highly militarized society under Castro. Massive military assistance from the former Soviet Union made this possible. Cuba's air force was the best equipped in Latin America in 1990. It had about 150 Soviet-supplied fighters, including advanced MiG-23 Floggers and MiG-29 Fulcrums. Cuba's military buildup peaked in the early 1990s, when its armed forces reached 235,000 regular troops.

Almost all aid for Cuba's military disappeared after the Soviet Union broke up in 1991. The Revolutionary Armed Forces (Spanish acronym FAR) was down to 60,000 regular troops in 2001. The army reserves had another 39,000 troops. Many of the island's citizens were involved in semiofficial military groups. These included the Civil Defense Force (50,000), the Youth Labor Army (65,000), and Territorial Militia Troops (1,000,000).

U.S. intelligence agencies report that Cuba's military readiness has decreased since the fall of the Soviet Union. In addition to reductions in active manpower, the FAR has a large portion of its heavy equipment, such as tanks, trucks, and planes, in storage. Most of the stored equipment is unavailable on short notice and cannibalized for spare parts to keep active duty equipment operating. Cuba no longer has any functioning submarines and only about a dozen of its remaining surface vessels are combat capable. Additionally, only 24 MiG jets are operational among the 150 Soviet-supplied fighter planes.

The FAR must now grow its own food and raise money to pay for some of its own expenses. Significant numbers of active duty forces are devoted to agricultural, business, and manufacturing activities that help feed the troops and generate revenues.

Although the strength of the military has declined in recent years, Cuba still has two units of highly trained Special Troops that assist in security and special operations.

Cuba still maintains two battalions of Special Troops. Together they include 2,000 personnel. These units are smaller than they were when the Soviet Union dissolved, but they can still perform special military and internal security missions. These battalions are part of the official structure of the Ministry of the Interior, and they are the most highly trained of all Cuba's military personnel. Special Troops utilize light weaponry and explosives. Their original mission was to provide for the personal security of Fidel Castro. They have also carried out special operations in Castro's wars of liberation.

Police State

Most Communist countries become police states, as Communism emphasizes requirements of the state rather than individual freedoms. A police state purposely uses its police force (and its military) to keep people from expressing their dissatisfaction and to stay in power. In Cuba, any expression of displeasure at the loss of freedom or any defiance of the Communist system can lead to arrest and punishment by a fine, imprisonment, banishment, or execution. The Cuban police and Communist Party authorities routinely harass, threaten, imprison, and humiliate defiant citizens.

Trials are unfair and usually over in less than one day. There are no jury trials. Trials of political dissidents are not open to the public. Often the only evidence against a defendant is the defendant's confession. The police usually obtain it by the use of force or threats during interrogation. Suspects often do not have legal advice from a lawyer. The defendant usually does not see his or her lawyer until the day of the trial. Prisoners die in jail due to a lack of medical care. Members of security forces and prison officials beat and otherwise abuse detainees and prisoners.

The government also infringes on citizens' privacy rights. It denies citizens the freedoms of speech and press. Merely expressing views that are at odds with those of the government can bring sentences of up to 14 years. Journalists can be given prison terms of up to 20 years for "disseminating literature deemed subversive." The government punishes any unauthorized assembly of more than three persons by up to three months in prison and a fine. The authorities selectively enforce this punishment and often use it to harass and imprison human rights advocates.

The government organizes Communist Party members into block committees. Block committees watch for suspicious activities in their neighborhoods. Examples of suspicious activities are spending lots of money, unauthorized meetings with foreign visitors, and defiant attitudes toward the government. The Interior Ministry's Department of State Security controls all access to the Internet. All electronic mail messages are subject to censorship. The ministry also reads international correspondence. It monitors all overseas telephone calls, and it even monitors domestic phone calls and correspondence.

The government also monitors the distribution of foreign publications and news, reserving them for selected faithful party members. It maintains strict censorship of news and information to the public. It also severely restricts workers' rights, including the right to form independent unions. Although the government prohibits forced labor by children, it requires children to do farm work for no pay (see Chapter 7, "Living In Cuba Today").

Fidel Castro

A popular story about Fidel Castro describes a speech that he gave outdoors in Havana on a cool evening in January 1959. It was just 10 days after the Cuban Revolution ended. Castro spoke to a throng of 40,000 people. Just as he began to speak, supporters released three white doves. Rather than soaring upward and disappearing into the night sky, as one would expect, two of them landed on the speaker's podium. The third floated gently onto Castro's shoulder and stayed there, fluttering its wings to keep its balance. The moment seemed perfect: the hero of Cuba surrounded by doves of peace. For many Cubans who remain on the island today and who can remember life under Batista, this image of Castro as liberator and symbol of hope is as strong today as it was then.

This story reveals an important reason for Castro's absolute power in Cuba today: Many Cubans still consider him a hero. He is also a powerful speaker and charismatic leader. He is famous for giving long speeches that "exert a mystical hold over the Cuban masses." Warren Hinckle and William W. Turner, authors of *The Fish Is Red: The Story of the Secret War Against Castro*, describe Castro as a man who can outtalk anyone in Cuba. They say that Fidel is the "kind of man who, when asked if he owned a dog, would go into rhapsodies of detail about the dog's size and color, his pedigree, the tricks he knew, his intelligence, his hunting ability, his house brokenness; whereas

Raúl, if asked the same question, would say, '*Sí*, I have a dog.'"

Fidel Castro was born in 1926 on his family's prosperous sugar plantation near Birán in the former Oriente Province. (Birán is in Holguín Province now.) Castro went to a Jesuit college in Havana where he was an all-around athlete; he played basketball, he was an above average baseball pitcher, and for a while he held the school record for the 800-meter run. He graduated from college in 1947 near the head of his class. One of Castro's teachers saw his leadership qualities and wrote prophetically in Castro's yearbook that he was "made of the stuff of heroes. A statue will be sculptured of you and the history of your country will speak your name."

We know little about Castro's private life. He was married and divorced before the revolution. He has a daughter from that marriage. Both mother and daughter live in Spain and do not wish to see him or speak with him. Since his divorce, reports link him to only one other woman, Celia Sanchez. A heroine of the revolution, she played a central role in the rebel underground. She waited for Castro in the Sierra Maestra while he was in exile in Mexico preparing for his return to Cuba. Sanchez fought by his side. She was probably Castro's closest adviser until she died from cancer in 1980.

Castro has reserved a place in history as Cuba's most charismatic leader and as the founder of the first and perhaps last Communist government in the Western Hemisphere. In 1997, the then 71-year-old Castro designated his younger brother Raúl as his successor. However, Raúl is only five years younger than Fidel and not a popular figure like his brother. Moreover, economic discontent on the island is spreading. A common question in Cuba as the 21st century unfolds is "What will Cuba's economy be like after Fidel"?

This notice informs citizens that the amount of bread that can be purchased is limited. The government rations food and other goods. Shortages at state-run stores are common.

Economy

Socialism

The Castro government transformed the Cuban economy from capitalism to Marxist-Leninist socialism. The main element of Marxist-Leninist socialism is the government's "nationalization of all means of production." This phrase means that the government takes over ownership of all farms, factories, warehouses, railroads, banks, and so on. The government also sets all prices, wages, and salaries and plans all economic activity. The goal of Marxist-Leninist socialism is to transform society into a classless society in which all workers contribute equal labor and receive equal pay. A one-party, Communist political system leads a nation toward this goal, according to Marxist-Leninist theory. Communists refer to the "Revolution" as the process that brings forth a classless society.

Socialism in this extreme form is the opposite of capitalism.

Capitalism promotes profit making by individuals, pricing of goods based on their supply and demand, and earning of wages and salaries based on effort, skill, and education.

Trade with the Soviet Union

Cuba's economy was in a shambles immediately after the revolution. The Castro government confiscated American bank accounts and his agrarian and industrial reforms took away property from Americans. Understandably, these policies drove away American investments, which had bolstered Batista's economy by creating jobs for Cubans. Moreover, the United States, Cuba's greatest customer for its sugar, slapped an embargo on American businesses trading with the island. The Organization of American States (composed of the United States and most Latin American countries) did the same thing. The embargoes made Cuba's economic situation even worse. Without hard cash from trade, no money was available to pay for repairing the roads, bridges, and factories damaged during the revolution.

Castro replaced the U.S. economic dominance of Cuba with that of the Soviet Union. In the early 1960s, he turned to the European Communist bloc, which included the Soviet Union and its European satellites (Poland, Romania, Czechoslovakia, and Hungary), for assistance. Since Cuba was short on cash, the bloc traded with Cuba using a barter system, which means to trade for something without money. Cuba traded its sugar for oil, food, and raw materials.

The Soviet Union and Cuba manipulated this system. The Soviet Union made its payments for sugar in oil and other commodities at prices well below what they could get in the world market. In other words, the Soviet Union was taking a financial loss to subsidize Cuba's fragile economy. Cuba often resold Soviet oil for hard currency at the higher, world market price. The Castro government then used the oil money to finance expensive construction projects and social programs.

Estimates of the amount of money Cuba earned by reselling oil range in the billions of dollars annually.

The Soviet Union's motive for making such a deal was to make Cuba dependent on it economically. The ultimate goal of the Soviet scheme was to gain a strategic foothold in the Western Hemisphere. (Long-range guided missiles launched from Cuba could reach anywhere in the United States.) Castro's government went along because it got hard cash and badly needed fuel for tractors, cars, and factories. Besides, Castro was leaning toward a Soviet style political system by this time anyway. The Soviet Union became Cuba's most important trading partner; it purchased 81 percent of Cuba's exports and provided 66 percent of its imports by 1990. The Soviet assistance through the barter system meant that Cuba had large amounts of cash and did not particularly need any foreign investment.

Collapse of Soviet Trade

The barter of commodities for sugar ended abruptly when the Soviet Union collapsed in 1991. Soviet trade could no longer subsidize Cuba. Since then, the island has traded solely on a cash basis at market prices. Price inflation has ravaged the economy. Costs of energy, consumer goods, and food have been rising steadily since supplies from the Soviet Union dried up. In addition, the island has continued to suffer the effects of the U.S. trade embargo.

The shortage of fuel has shut down some factories and has slowed production in others. City dwellers rely on bicycles for transportation due to the scarcity of gasoline. Many farm workers, in the absence of gasoline, tractor parts, and tires, now transport their crops by ox-drawn cart.

The island also faces a serious food shortage. Cuba was importing 40 percent of its food from the Soviet Union when it collapsed. The government issues ration cards (*libretas*) for food and other consumer goods that the cardholder can pick up at state stores (*bodegas*). A typical card allots small amounts of basic foods to the holder free or at a very low cost each month: about 1 pound (2.5 kilograms) of rice, 2/3 pound (1.5 kilograms) of sugar, 1/5 pound (1/2 kilogram) of beans, and 14 eggs. Everyone is supposed to receive one bread roll each day. The card allots other essential items, including clothing, toothpaste, and soap. There are also small amounts of vegetable oil for cooking, salt, coffee, crackers, canned tomatoes, and fruits and vegetables. The stores hand out small quantities of meat only once or twice a year.

There are always long lines of people waiting to pick up their food. Unfortunately, the state stores are often out of items listed on the card. Moreover, the amounts are quite small. No one survives solely on the ration card. Some people sell personal items, such as jewelry and family heirlooms, to buy food.

James Michener, the famous writer and coauthor of *Six Days in Havana*, quotes a local citizen standing in line with his ration card outside a bodega: "Don't let them [government officials] tell you the American embargo accomplishes nothing. It's strangling the flow of our consumer goods." Another informant told him, "For the past six months, no toilet paper of any kind. No toothpaste, same time. No cosmetics for young women, not of any kind for the past year and a half." Since the Soviet Union's collapse, living standards are falling and an increasing number of Cubans are seeking to emigrate.

Fidelismo

The Cuban people refer to Castro's strict brand of socialism as "Fidelismo." In 1993, faced with a shortage of hard currency in the economy, Castro said that "life, reality . . . forces us to do what we would have never done otherwise . . . we must make concessions." The concessions to which he referred involved temporarily abandoning principles of the "Revolution" and tolerating capitalistic (profit-taking) influences. There have been five basic adjustments to Fidelismo since then.

First, Cuban citizens are now allowed to receive U.S. dollars in the mail from relatives in the capitalist United States. Cubans had been using these dollars to purchase expensive foreign goods in Cuba's black market. Since 1994, the government has allowed its citizens to spend U.S. dollars in special state-owned dollar stores. Using dollars legally provides the Cuban economy with much needed hard currency and it reduces people's need to trade on the black market.

Second, in 1993, the government converted many big state-owned farms into cooperatives whose members set their own goals and share in profits. In addition, the government gave permission to urban dwellers to organize cooperatives on underutilized land on remaining state farms. Today, urban-based cooperatives cultivate vegetables and other basic food crops. They farm 42 percent of Cuba's arable land. Farmers from state farms and urban-based cooperatives now sell part of their production to the public in farmers markets (*agromercados*) and set their prices in U.S. dollars.

Third, the Castro government now encourages joint business ventures. Joint ventures are profit-seeking partnerships between the government and foreign businesses. The government is using these partnerships to revive and diversify the manufacturing sector of the economy. Cuba's educated and skilled labor force and low wage rates are attractive to foreign companies. Joint ventures are also heavily involved in the construction and management of luxury, state-owned tourist hotels.

Fourth, the government adjusted its own budget. It cut its subsidies to state-owned enterprises (80 percent of which were operating at a loss); raised prices on cigarettes, gasoline, alcohol, electricity, and other goods and services; and for the first time since the revolution, established a tax system.

Fifth, to meet demand for more services, the Castro government legalized self-employment in more than 170 different occupations that range from auto mechanics to hairdressers. These new businesspeople can charge whatever the market for their services will bring. Tourists see the most noticeable examples of these new businesses—small bed and breakfasts (*casas particulares*) and privately operated family restaurants (*paladares*).

The opportunity for self-employment has drawn hundreds of thousands of workers into this new sector of the economy. The government gets its share of the money spent on these services through a combination of monthly fees and income taxes. Unfortunately, the list of occupations does not include professions requiring university degrees. Consequently, educated people, such as professors and doctors, moonlight for extra income in better paying self-employed jobs or in the tourism industry.

The adjustments of Fidelismo are a long way from permanent, however. They depend on what Fidel Castro decides he wants. Thus, in Havana, in February 2002, the Castro government declared hundreds of self-employed operators of food stalls, street vendors, restaurants, and bed and breakfasts "unauthorized" to practice their businesses. Police suddenly appeared and closed many of them down. Some observers believe this action was another of Castro's "capitalist" adjustments, as these small businesses were selling food to tourists and thereby cutting into the profits of restaurants in government-owned tourist hotels.

As the 21st century unfolds, Cuba's economy seems to be on an uncertain course. As one journalist describes the beneficiaries of Fidelismo, "Like the boat people who still leave Cuba's shores, these would-be capitalists are the 'land rafters' of the socialist economy, embarking on a perilous and uncertain journey."

Trade Today

Today, Russia is the most important buyer of the island's exports. Cuba spends more money buying goods from Spain than any other country. The Organization of American States abandoned multilateral sanctions against Cuba in 1975. Mexico, Venezuela, Jamaica, and Colombia are Cuba's main Latin American trading partners.

The sugar industry has been adversely affected by environmental conditions such as hurricanes and drought. In addition, the industry suffered a setback when the Soviet Union stopped trading its oil for Cuban sugar.

Cuba's main exports are sugar, nickel, tobacco, fish, fruit, and coffee. The island has had a trade deficit ever since the collapse of the Soviet Union. A trade deficit occurs when the value of imports is greater than that of exports. The value of imports (almost $3.3 billion) was about twice that of exports in 1998 (over $1.7 billion).

Cuba's GDP and Average Income

The U.S. Central Intelligence Agency (CIA) calculates a country's average income based on its gross domestic product (GDP). The GDP is the value of all final goods and services produced within a country in a given year. The average income is the income that each person in a country would have if each citizen were to receive an even share of the GDP.

According to the *World Fact Book,* a CIA publication, Cuba, in 2000, had a GDP of $19.2 billion and an average income of $1,700. The average income is lower than any other Caribbean country (Table 4). However, unlike the other countries of the region, Cuba's Communist government provides many items to its citizens at a low cost, such as subsidized rent, health care, and some basic foodstuffs with ration cards. The average Cuban spends less on these items, and consequently, has more money to spend on other items. Even so, the adjusted average income for the island rises to only $3,700.

Table 4: Per Capita Incomes of Caribbean Island Countries

COUNTRY	AVERAGE INCOME (U.S. DOLLARS)*
Aruba	28,000
Cayman Islands	24,500
Bahamas, The	15,000
Barbados	14,500
Netherlands Antilles (other than Aruba)	11,400
Puerto Rico	10,000
Trinidad and Tobago	9,500
Antigua and Barbuda	8,200
St. Kitts and Nevis	7,000
Dominican Republic	5,700
St. Lucia	4,500
Grenada	4,400
Dominica	4,000
Jamaica	3,700
St. Vincent and Grenadines	2,800
Haiti	1,800
Cuba	**1,700**

* Incomes are based on 2000 estimates of the GDP.
  Source: Central Intelligence Agency, 2001.

Cuba's economy has been improving slowly since the mid-1990s. The annual increase in consumer prices (rate of inflation) has been lower than even the most advanced countries. The rate of inflation was only 0.3 percent in 2000. The production and sale of goods and services has also been improving. Annual changes in the GDP indicate this improvement, as it has been rising steadily each year since the mid-1990s.

Table 5 shows a percentage breakdown of Cuba's GDP according to economic activity. Primary industries use natural land resources to produce goods and services. They include agricultural, fishing, forestry, mining, electrical, gas, and water industries. These industries employ about 25 percent of the labor force. Secondary industries add value to goods and services

Table 5: Percentage of Gross Domestic Product, 1990-2000

ECONOMIC ACTIVITY	1990	2000	CHANGE
Primary Industries			
Agriculture, Fishing, and Forestry	9.3	7.5	-1.8
Mining	0.5	1.3	+0.8
Electrical, gas, and water	7.9	4.2	+3.7
Secondary Industries			
Manufacturing	24.4	29.0	+4.6
Construction	2.4	2.9	+0.5
Services			
Trade, restaurants, and hotels	26.0	21.5	-4.5
Transportation and communications	6.3	6.0	-0.3
Financial institutions and real estate	3.2	4.0	+0.8
Community, social, and personal services	20.0	23.6	+3.6
Total	**100.0**	**100.0**	

Sources: Government of Cuba (www.cubagob.cu) for 1990 data and Government of India for 2000 data (www.indembassyhavana.cu)

produced by primary industries. The processing of raw materials from Cuba's farms, seaports, and mines account for 84 percent of Cuba's exports. Secondary industries include manufacturing and construction. They employ about 24 percent of the labor force. Service industries provide services to people. They include the huge bureaucracy of state-owned enterprises and employ 51 percent of the labor force.

Manufacturing

The Castro government confiscated all factories when it took over the island. The government placed production under the control of large state bureaucracies. The breakup of the Soviet Union in 1991 ended the importation of cheap raw materials for factories. The Cuban government had to close the factories and lay off thousands of workers. Many of the workers now work as manual laborers in the countryside.

Despite the layoffs, manufacturing accounted for 29 percent of the GDP in 2000. Cuban factories produce leather goods, textiles, plastics, cement, clothing, and numerous everyday items ranging from cosmetics and perfumes to mattresses and toiletries. Sugar mills are one of the largest employers in the manufacturing sector.

Agriculture

The island's low population density and favorable combination of climate, topography, and soils make it especially suitable for agriculture. About one-fourth of the land is arable (suitable for producing crops). Cuba's principle agricultural crops are sugarcane, tobacco, citrus, and coffee. Agriculture (along with fishing and forestry) was responsible for 7.5 percent of the GNP in 2000 (Table 5). This figure gives the false impression that agriculture is not very important to the economy: it does not include the income generated by the manufacture of agricultural products, such as sugar—the country's main and most valuable export item.

Sugarcane accounts for about 40 percent of the value of all exports. Diego Velázquez, Cuba's first Spanish governor introduced sugarcane in the town of Baracoa. Cuba is one of the world's major exporters of cane sugar. More than one half of the island's cultivated land is devoted to this crop. The manufacture of sugar from cane is the chief product. By-products include molasses, syrups, industrial alcohol from molasses, and rum. The cane harvest occurs during the dry season, from January through April.

Despite sugarcane's importance relative to other crops, its production is a shadow of what it used to be. Peak years of production occurred when the Soviet Union traded oil for Cuban sugar. When the Soviet Union collapsed in 1991, sugar exports fell dramatically. For example, exports in 1999 were 34 percent below 1990 levels.

The Soviet practice of paying for Cuban sugar at world market prices hid inefficiencies from field to factory. These inefficiencies were to blame for a general 40-year decline in yields: laborers were harvesting both mature and young cane plants indiscriminately, and old and obsolete equipment was operating in most sugar mills. A severe three-year (1997-2000) drought in eastern Cuba and crop damage caused by Hurricane Georges in 1998 and Hurricane Michelle in 2001 added to the industry's woes.

The government recently took steps to rescue the sugarcane industry by improving harvesting methods, closing inefficient plants, and consolidating better equipment in remaining plants. Yields appear to be rising. Cuba's red clay soils and plains areas in Matanzas, Villa Clara, and Sancti Spíritus provinces have the greatest concentrations of sugarcane fields. Few areas in Cuba do not cultivate sugarcane; such areas include the Zapata Peninsula, the Isla de la Juventud, and the island's mountain ranges.

Tobacco is a New World crop. The Arawak Indians smoked it for ceremonial purposes. Tobacco is the second most valuable crop in Cuba; it accounts for about 10 percent of the total value of the country's exports. Cuban tobacco is famous worldwide for its hand-rolled luxury cigars. Tobacco farms (*vegas*) produce the finest cigar tobacco in western Pinar del Río Province, in an area called Vuelta Abajo, and in the Partidos areas in central Havana Province. Laborers pick the tobacco leaves by hand and store the harvested leaves in drying sheds. These sheds (*casas de tabaco*) have tall steeply pitched, thatched roofs and dot the landscape of tobacco growing areas.

Cuba exports more than one million cigars annually. Castro was famous for always having a cigar in his hand or mouth. He gave up smoking cigars in the 1980s, explaining wisely: "They are good for the country, but not so good for your health."

Citrus fruits, such as grapefruits and oranges, are Cuba's third most important agricultural export. Cuba had preferential trading agreements with the Eastern European Communist bloc for its citrus production. Citrus production peaked in the late 1980s, but the end of these agreements in the early 1990s caused output to plummet by 50 percent. The export value of citrus fruits accounted for about 3 percent of the total value of exports in 1998. The island's other fruits include pineapples and bananas. Farmers grow pineapples for commercial purposes in central Camagüey Province. Typically, rural dwellers grow banana plants and mango trees near homes for their shade and succulent fruit.

A French coffee grower fleeing the Haitian rebellion brought coffee to Cuba in the late 18th century. Coffee is a mountain crop, and growing areas are very picturesque. Short-sleeved farmers, their faces shaded by broad brimmed hats, pick the red coffee berries by hand. They load heavy sacks of berries onto mules and transport them to collection points. Small processing plants remove the pulp from the berries and sun dry the beans.

The regions of highest yield are the Escambray Mountains in south central Cuba and in the Sierra Maestra and the

Workers carry harvested tobacco leaves to the drying shed. Hand-rolled cigars are a major export and are known for their exceptional quality.

Baracoa massif area in southeastern Cuba.

A government program started in 1994 to resettle people in abandoned coffee farms (*fincas*) in the mountains of eastern Cuba is responsible for a resurgence of production there, which is for domestic consumption. Coffee is a popular drink among Cubans, as it is among Americans.

Mining

An ore is a concentration of metallic minerals in rock. Mining is the process that extracts (separates out) the ore from the rock. Cuba has several mineral ores: nickel, cobalt, chromite, copper, gold, tungsten, manganese, and iron. Rock formations in the island's mountainous areas contain deposits (concentrations) of the ores. Mining was responsible for 1.3 percent of Cuba's GDP in 2000.

Cuba has 37 percent of the world's nickel reserves. No other country has such a large supply. It was the sixth largest producer of mined nickel in the world in 1998. Cobalt, which is a by-product of nickel operations, is also important to Cuba's mineral sector. In 1998, Cuba was the fifth leading producer of cobalt, with an output of about 9 percent of the total world production. Metal scientists (metallurgists) use nickel in batteries and in plating (covering in a thin layer) other metals that are prone to erode chemically. Doctors use the radioactive property of cobalt to treat cancer patients. Metallurgists mix small quantities of the metal with aluminum oxides to make a dark-blue pigment for inks, paints, and varnishes. Metal scientists also use cobalt in high-strength alloys (combinations of metals).

Nickel ranks second after sugar as an export commodity. The reserves and mines are concentrated along the coast of eastern Holguín Province. Two large nickel-processing plants operate in the area. U.S. companies built these plants during World War II. Engineers from the Soviet Union expanded the plants using inefficient technology, after Castro's government confiscated them in 1960. These plants are still operating.

A Canadian company, as part of a joint venture with the Cuban government, ships nearly all the island's nickel to Canada for smelting. Because of Canadian investments, nickel exports are at record levels. They earned $380 million in 1998. Canadian mining companies have become involved in developing Cuba's mining potential since 1991.

Small mines yield copper (for making wire) and manganese (for making wear resistant alloys of copper and iron). The mines are in Pinar del Río and Santiago de Cuba provinces. (The Western Hemisphere's oldest copper mine is near the city of Santiago de Cuba.) There is a chromite mine in Holguín Province. Chromite is the source of the mineral chromium. Plating chromium onto another metal makes such things as shiny car hubcaps and bumpers. Mixing it with steel creates stainless steel flatware, such as knives, spoons, and forks.

Miners in Pinar del Río and Cienfuegos provinces quarry limestone. Cement plants crush the limestone and make it into lime powder and cement. Sugar mills use burned lime powder to separate sugarcane pulp from sugar juice. Many sugar mills operate their own limestone quarries and limekilns. Lime makes mortar and plaster, as well as fertilizer. Various manufacturing processes use it in making paper, textiles, and soap. Cuban miners also mine small amounts of gold (for jewelry and dentistry), silica sand (for making glass), and gypsum (for making plaster of Paris and cement).

Geologists did not discover Cuba's main oil field until 1981. The delay was due, in part, to Cuba's supply of cheap oil from the Soviet Union. In the absence of Soviet oil since 1991, foreign investments are boosting domestic oil drilling, exploration, and refining. The government has several joint ventures involved in drilling and exploring for more oil. Cuba's partners in these ventures are companies from Brazil, Canada, France, Spain, Sweden, and the United Kingdom. Production is for domestic use and accounts for about one-fifth of the nation's total consumption. Venezuela and Mexico supply most of Cuba's importation needs.

Oil production is at record levels. Nearly all of the oil is currently coming from a field stretching between Havana and Cárdenas. Refineries in Havana, Cienfuegos, and Santiago de Cuba convert the thick crude oil into usable products such as motor oil, gasoline, diesel, kerosene, and sulfur.

Fishing

Before the 1959 revolution, Cuba's commercial fishing industry fished the island's shore waters and deeper waters of the Gulf of Mexico and Caribbean Sea. The catch included a complement of reef fish (snapper and grouper); spiny lobster; sponge in shore fisheries; and mackerel, tuna, and billfish in deep-water fisheries. Most fishing was for the Cuban market.

After the revolution, the Cuban fishing industry became an

important supplier of seafood products for the world market. The Castro government used money from resold Soviet oil to purchase expensive, deep-water fishing boats. However, in the late 1970s, most nations in the Western Hemisphere imposed 200-mile limits for territorial waters. This policy was not a protest against Castro's politics; it was part of a general movement among nations to claim resources of the sea. Nevertheless, the 200-mile limit denied Cuba access to most of the Gulf of Mexico and Caribbean waters.

Cuban fleets had to operate in more distant, deeper waters in the Atlantic and Pacific Oceans as a result. Open ocean fishing is more expensive: fuel costs are higher and catches of deep-water fish (mackerels, herrings, and hake) bring low prices per unit of volume. The high seas fleet was almost totally shut down in the 1990s when Cuba stopped importing Soviet fuel. As a result, Cuba's total fish catch in 1997 was 56 percent below that of 1986.

Forty major processing plants freeze, smoke, salt, and package a variety of seafood products for sale at home and abroad. The shore fleet still plays an important role in providing seafood to the Cuban people. Part of the catch goes to Asia (particularly Japan), Canada, Europe, and Latin America.

The seafood industry accounts for 7 percent of Cuba's exports. Havana is the most important fishing port. Important secondary ports are Surgidero de Bataban, Santa Cruz del Sur, and Manzanillo. Tuna and hake are the most important species taken in deeper waters. Fisheries in waters closer to shore provide good yields of shrimp, lobster, and red snapper.

Tourism

Cuba was the first Caribbean nation to attract tourists. In the mid-1950s, virtually every North American who traveled to the region chose Cuba as their only destination. More than 270,000 Americans were coming to the island each year. Due to U.S. economic sanctions, American tourists stopped coming after Castro took power. The U.S. government's ban on U.S. tourists going to Cuba in 1961 made Caribbean destinations such as Jamaica much more popular.

Cuba's warm temperatures, scenic cultural and physical landscapes, and shear size make this island a tourist agent's dream. In 1988, as political and economic problems began to mount in the Soviet Union, Cuban officials decided to establish a tourism office for the first time and an increase in tourism took place almost overnight.

Tourism replaced sugar exports as Cuba's main source of foreign exchange in the mid-1990s. The growth in this industry has been astounding. The number of visitors that Cuba has received has grown from 340,300 visitors in 1990 to 1.7 million visitors in 2000—a fivefold increase. Cuba collected more than $1.9 million from tourists in 2000, which was 14 percent of all government revenues that year.

Havana and the beach resort capital Varadero have well-developed tourism infrastructures with luxury hotels and restaurants. Cuba is engaged in joint ventures to develop tourism in Cayo Coco and Cayo Guillermo along the island's north coast. Cuban officials are planning for the arrival of almost seven million tourists in the year 2010. They note, however, that Europeans would make up 65 percent of this figure; with the remainder coming from Canada and Latin America. Cuban officials suggest that the total number of guests could increase dramatically if the market opened to Americans, who are a short plane ride away.

The capital city of Havana is the center of commerce, industry, politics, and culture. Spanish explorers originally settled the city in the early 1500s and used it as a trading center.

7

Living in Cuba Today

Urban Living

Seventy percent of Cuba's population lives in cities. Havana is the dominant urban center; one in four city dwellers live there. This metropolis of the Caribbean is a primate city, which means that Havana is huge in comparison to the size of the next largest city. Indeed, its population of almost 2.2 million is five times larger than Santiago de Cuba, Cuba's second largest city. Astonishingly, Havana is about as large as the combined populations of Cuba's next 12 largest cities. Table 6 lists the populations of Cuba's main cities.

Table 6: Population of Cuba's Main Cities (1993)

CITY	POPULATION
Havana City	2,175,888
Santiago de Cuba	430,494
Camagüey	294,332
Holguín	242,085
Guantánamo	207,796
Santa Clara	205,400
Bayamo	137,663
Cienfuegos	132,000
Pinar del Río	128,570
Las Tunas	126,930
Matanzas	122,588
Ciego de Ávila	95,500
Sancti Spíritus	93,800

*Note: Total population minus Havana City is 2,217,158
Source: United Nations Demographic Yearbook

Havana's population growth has slowed down markedly since the late 1960s. Emigration to the United States, sometimes with the encouragement of the government, has drawn people disproportionately from Havana. In recent years, the cities with the greatest percentage increases have been in the smaller cities of eastern Cuba: The cities of Bayamo, Holguín, and Las Tunas have moved up in the total population ranking.

Havana's primacy still dominates life in Cuba; it is the country's chief political, economic, and cultural center. It has long been strategically and commercially important because of its excellent harbor and its location on the Straits of Florida. Havana harbor is the main shipping point for agricultural exports, such as sugar, tobacco, and fruits. Imports passing through Havana include consumer durables, foodstuffs, cotton, machinery, and technical equipment.

Local industries include shipbuilding, light industries (mostly food processing and canning), and biotechnology. Assembly plants, rum distilleries, and factories making the famous Havana cigars are also important. As the island's most important hub of air and maritime transportation, this jewel of the Caribbean is famous for its colonial architecture. The Castro government revived tourism in Havana in the 1990s as part of the effort to replace the loss of subsidies from the Soviet Union.

Cuba's impoverished city dwellers live in grimy conditions. Paint and other maintenance materials are unavailable; garbage pickup is unreliable; cockroaches, flies, and gnats swarm in damp showers; and toilets only flush occasionally (water is often shut off in buildings due to the need for repairs). Elevators seldom work and electrical outages occur frequently (due to the shortage of imported oil for power generation). The government, which owns all property, simply does not have the money to pay for the maintenance costs.

Rural Living

Thirty percent of Cuba's population lives in rural towns and villages. Rural residents work in sugarcane, tobacco, or coffee plantations, or on cattle ranches. Hundreds of small fishing villages that line Cuba's coastline also qualify as rural. Rural settlement patterns have changed under Castro's dictatorship. The government has persuaded many scattered rural residents to work on larger state farms. The government has also resettled many workers from solitary huts to new rural towns. These towns have multistory, prefabricated apartment blocks built for an average of 250 families. The Communist government tries to provide the new towns with free running water, electricity, sewage disposal, schools, and medical services. Additionally, well-developed highway and railroad systems connect Cuba's major cities to the countryside. Nevertheless, these services suffer the same shortages as large cities do.

People in rural areas live in *bohiós*, which have thatched roofs and dirt floors. The villagers have some government services and have access to roads and transportation.

Before the Castro revolution, the gap between incomes of rural families and residents in cities was increasing. Few rural families could afford medical care, and rates of intestinal parasite infections, tuberculosis, and typhoid fever were much higher in rural areas. The Cuban agricultural worker's diet was deficient in protein and he or she weighed 16 pounds less than the national average. Meat and fish were rarely part of a rural worker's diet. Nineteen percent of the rural homes had electricity compared to 87 percent in urban homes. In an attempt to escape poverty, rural workers were moving to cities, especially to Havana, to find better paying jobs. This rural to urban migration was seriously overcrowding the capital, with three to five families crammed into single apartments.

The Castro government has stemmed the flow of emigration to Havana by several means. First, it kept investments in Havana low and gave priority to smaller cities and especially the country-side. The government also diverted new manufacturing activities away from Havana and into the countryside. Additionally, it established a rationing system, in part, to help equalize consumption in rural and urban areas. The government also trained and sent doctors to rural communities to improve medical care there. Moreover, it issued residence permits and worker's identity cards to inhibit internal migration flows to the capital.

The Plaza

Cuba's colonial cities and older rural towns share one common element—the plaza. Spanish colonists tried to recreate Spain's towns and cities in the New World. Thus, many of Cuba's settlements have Spanish plazas. Plazas are open-air squares in an urban setting. Cubans in many towns call their plazas *parques* (parks) because trees, shrubs, and flowers adorn them. Cuba's smaller colonial towns have a single plaza, which is always located in town centers. Larger towns usually have more than one plaza, with one central or main square and several smaller neighborhood plazas.

Plazas are centers of activity in the Cuban city. Major businesses, government offices, and cathedrals are on streets facing them or on nearby streets. The townspeople use these open spaces as gathering places for relaxation and conversations and for festivals, weddings, speeches, and other public and social activities. The plaza is easy to access from elsewhere in the city, as the Spaniards also included in their towns an orderly, rectangular grid of streets that enter plazas from all sides.

Plazas are centers of activity in the Cuban cities. Many, like the one shown here, have cathedrals or other large buildings on the streets facing them. These plazas were an attempt by the Spanish colonists to re-create the ambience of the towns and cities in the Old World.

U.S. Naval Station, Guantánamo Bay

Not everyone living on the island of Cuba is actually living in Cuban territory. By virtue of the Platt Amendment, the United States acquired a permanent lease on a 45-square-mile area on the island's eastern tip in 1903 (see chapter 3, "History"). A U.S. naval station was built at the site. The base, the U.S. Naval Station at Guantánamo Bay, is 12 miles south of the city of Guantánamo. Over the years, the United States has used "Gitmo," as the base personnel call it, as a base for military support and special operations in Cuba, Nicaragua, Guatemala, Honduras, El Salvador, Panama, and Grenada.

In recent years, U.S. authorities have used the naval station to detain refugees who have attempted to enter the United States without permission. U.S. immigration officials allow those refugees to enter the United States as legal immigrants if their government would persecute them for their political beliefs. U.S. officials repatriate refugees (send them back to their home countries), if they are not political refugees.

In 1991 a coup in nearby Haiti sent refugees by sea toward the United States. The U.S. Navy and U.S. Coast Guard picked up about 10,000 refugees before they reached U.S. shores. The refugees stayed at Guantánamo for processing. Guantánamo was also the detention center for 60,000 more refugees after huge boatlifts from Haiti and Cuba in 1994. The North American Treaty Organization (NATO) authorities once considered the base as a destination center for about 20,000 refugees from Kosovo. (Kosovo is a state in the country of Serbia, which is in Eastern Europe). NATO never carried out this plan.

The United States is now using Gitmo as a detention and interrogation center for terrorists in the War on Terrorism. The United States and its allies declared the unofficial war after terrorists attacked and destroyed the World Trade Center towers in New York on September 11, 2001. The war is against all terrorist organizations and the countries that aid or harbor them. In 2002 the naval station had 2,000 members of the Taliban and al-Qaeda taken prisoner in Afghanistan. The Taliban is a group of religious extremists that ruled Afghanistan and harbored members of al-Qaeda, an international terrorist organization. Undoubtedly more terrorists and their protectors from other parts of the world will be living at the U.S. Naval Station at Guantánamo as long as the American-led War on Terrorism continues.

Air Travel

Since the early 1990s, the Castro government has encouraged foreign airlines to make Cuba a destination. Consequently, despite the U.S. efforts to isolate Cuba, aircraft link the country very well to global tourist and business markets: more than 20 foreign airlines fly regularly to the island and almost all visitors arrive by air. Additionally, direct charter flights enter from Canada, the Caribbean, Central and South America and Europe. There are even occasional charter flights from the United States. Cuba Airways (Cubana de Aviacin), the main state-owned airline, also flies visitors into the country. The main airport is the José Martí International Airport, located about 13 miles from Havana.

Cuba Airways operates most flights inside Cuba. It caters to both visitors and Cubans. The are domestic flights between Havana and several other cities: Baracoa, Bayamo, Camagüay, Ciego de Ávila, Guantánamo, Holguín, Las Tunas, Manzanillo, Moa, Nueva Gerona, Santiago de Cuba, and Varadero. The airline's planes are Soviet built. Most of them are 48-passenger propeller aircraft, although 120-passenger jets fly the longer routes between Havana and Bayamo, and Havana and Santiago de Cuba.

Unfortunately, Cuba Airways has the highest fatality rate per passenger in Latin America and the Caribbean. A second state-owned airline, Aerotaxi, has a fleet of smaller aircraft. It handles most of the shorter flights among Cuba's smaller airports.

Railroads and Highways

Cuba has the longest history of railroad passenger service in Latin America: It had the first passenger railroad in the region, which began operating in 1837. This track stretched just 23 miles (37 kilometers) between Havana and Bejucal, a small sugarcane town south of the capital. Since then, the island's railroad network has grown to include about 7,437 miles (11,969 kilometers) of track. This is enough track to crisscross the full length of the island nearly 10 times. However, most of the network consists of short spurs over which small steam locomotives haul cane from field to mill.

The state-owned Cuban Railroad (Ferrocarriles de Cuba) operates the rest of the tracks. The main axis of the network is the Cuban Central Railway, which runs from Havana to Santiago de Cuba. A Canadian company built this main track between 1900 and 1902. Castro nationalized it along with the rest of the island's railroads in 1961.

Few Cubans can afford to buy tickets for a train. Hence, the trains are less crowded and more relaxing than other forms of public transportation. There is usually at least one train a day on major routes. However, train service declined after the Soviet Union collapsed. Shortages of fuel and spare parts, aging equipment, and deteriorating tracks have been the main culprits. The tracks and equipment are so poor that top speeds are limited. Moreover, schedule cancellations are common, due to a shortage of fuel and mechanical problems.

Cuba's road network is among the best in Latin America. Cuban roads are in better condition because they have less traffic than other nations in the region. The most important road is the Central Highway (Carretera Central), built between 1926 and 1931. This two-lane road stretches from Pinar del Río to Guantánamo. Most large cities have bypass roads, so that drivers can avoid cities. The government began construction of an eight-lane National Freeway (Autopista Nacional) during the 1970s, when its coffers were flush from Soviet subsidies. This freeway is about half finished. It runs from Pinar del Río to Sancti Spíritus, with small sections around Santiago de Cuba and Guantánamo. Construction stopped in the late 1980s. The government was establishing a system of tolls on the major highways in 2002—another response to the government's need for hard currency. The government plans to use the toll money to pay for construction and maintenance of the island's roads.

Cars and Bicycles

Cubans drive on the right side of the road, as Americans do, and speed limits are similar to those in the United States: 25 miles per hour (40 kilometers per hour) in residential areas and around schools and 55 miles per hour (90 kilometers per hour) on freeways. Driving is more hazardous in rural areas: one must watch for slow-moving horse drawn carriages, ox carts, free-ranging animals, and tractors.

There were 125,000 registered passenger cars in Cuba in 1955. Most of them were American made, Chevrolets and Fords especially. Also popular were Buicks, Oldsmobiles, Plymouths, and Cadillacs. Hundreds, perhaps thousands, of cars stolen from the East Coast of the United States found their way to the island, owing to a car theft ring run by organized crime. A large number of these American cars are still operating in Cuba, mainly because Cubans are ingenious automobile mechanics. They have maintained thousands of vintage American cars from the heydays of the 1940s and 1950s. Typically, the cars' bodies and interior upholsteries are in incredibly good shape, however, their owners are unable to drive them much due to the shortage of gasoline.

Most Cubans use bicycles rather than cars to go to work and school or to run errands. The reliance on bicycles is another adaptation to the high cost of fuel brought on by the loss of Soviet subsidies. In the early 1990s, as soon as the fuel shortage took hold, the government imported more than 200,000 bicycles from China. Most families cannot afford multiple bicycles, so it is common to see a bicycle carrying two to four people. Whenever necessary, Cubans also carry odd loads, such as live animals (a pig or chickens secured in homemade cages) and firewood. The police allow cycling on freeways, because car and truck traffic is light. Cuba's flat to rolling terrain makes it easy to ride bicycles. Due to the high usage of bicycles, 37 percent of accidents on roads involved bicycles in 1997.

Hitchhiking is common in Cuba because many people cannot afford any other form of transportation. A law requires that drivers of government vehicles with empty seats pick up hitchhikers whenever they can. At major intersections and highway exits, government officials wearing yellow overalls flag down cars for hitchhiking Cubans. There is usually a line of hitchhikers waiting their turn at these places.

Buses, Trucks, Horse Carts, and Bicitaxis

Most Cubans rely on various means of cheap public transportation. They depend heavily on state-owned buses to travel between cities. Cuba's government bus service links all provincial capitals and many satellite towns once or twice daily. Many provincial capitals have two bus stations: a station for local buses traveling within the provinces and a station for traveling between provinces.

Unfortunately, buses are rare because many government-owned buses have stopped running for the lack of spare parts and gasoline. Consequently, buses that do operate are crowded. There are a few air-conditioned buses, but these are expensive. Only tourists, rich businesspeople, and Communist Party and government officials can afford to ride them.

As a practical matter, a "capitalistic" adjustment of Fidelismo has been to allow privately owned trucks (*camiones particulares*) to participate in the business of intercity passenger transportation. These passenger trucks are more common in eastern Cuba. They have big, open-sided flat beds with benches. A metal bar or wood frame, to which a rolled up canvas roof is attached, arches over the bed. Passengers unroll the canvas roof for protection when it rains. The trucks are always full, as they are the only means of public transportation between small rural towns.

For short trips within towns, privately operated horse carts follow fixed routes. Bicitaxis, which are large tricycles with a double seat behind the driver, are a common means of conveyance in Cuba's larger cities. The horse cart and bicitaxi operators are on the list of Castro's 170 acceptable "capitalist" occupations.

Food and Dress

"Do you know what most Cubans think about when they wake up in the morning? What am I going to eat?" This quote by Catherine Moses, author of *Real Life in Castro's Cuba*, captures the stark reality about what Cubans eat. They eat whatever is available and affordable to them. A complete traditional Cuban meal is only something tourists experience nowadays. Such dishes usually include white rice (arroz) and red or black beans (frijoles). Another common ingredient is beef or pork brazed with onions in olive oil on a hot skillet. Root vegetables are also a popular part of Cuban meals, particularly manioc (yucca or cassava) and *boniato*, a kind of sweet potato.

No matter what the meal, Cubans like to garnish their food with garlic, cumin, oregano, parsley, sour oranges, peppers, and other spices. A soupy stew of black beans (*potaje*) served alongside plain white rice is a common dish. Desserts consist of fruit (often with some combination of mango, banana, and pineapple) and ice cream.

Cubans usually dress informally. The island's mild temperatures enable them to wear casual summer clothing all year, with only a sweater or light jacket for winter. The men prefer to wear the *guayabera*, originally the cotton or linen work shirt of the rural worker, and light cotton pants. On formal occasions, such as on national holidays, official dinners, and receptions, men wear lightweight suits. Women wear either long dresses or shorter styles for dinners and receptions. They never wear hats, gloves, or stockings. Slacks or a lightweight dress is acceptable attire for office work. Children wear shorts or lightweight pants year-round. All types of shoes and sandals are acceptable. Cubans wear T-shirts and sneakers or athletic shoes for recreational activities.

Practically all clothing comes from local factories and is of poor quality. Imported items are too expensive for most people.

Health Care

The provision of universal health care is a triumph of the revolution, according to Fidel Castro. He often cites in his speeches the fact that Cuba has the lowest infant mortality rate in Latin America. However, Cuba also had the lowest infant mortality rate in Latin America and the 13th lowest rate in the world in 1957, before Castro came to power. Cuba ranked ahead of France, Belgium, West Germany, Israel, Japan, Austria, Italy, Spain, and Portugal. Moreover, the infant mortality rankings of all these countries dropped below Cuba's since Castro took office. Also missing from the government's ranking of infant mortality is a staggering abortion rate (0.71 abortions per live birth in 1991). Abortions include termination of high-risk pregnancies and therefore lower the number of infant deaths.

The government has not lived up to its promise of a quality health care system. The system worked well because Soviet subsidies financed clinics, hospitals, and the training of doctors. The system has been deteriorating markedly ever since the subsidies disappeared in 1991. Basic medical supplies have all but evaporated. Even essentials, such as disinfectants and soap, are in short supply. Moreover, thousands of Cuba's doctors have left the island in the past decade because the health care system is so inadequate.

Castro's socialism also provides an inadequate food supply without Soviet subsidies. The per capita daily caloric consumption is a good indicator of the general health of a population. The more calories of energy that are consumed, the greater resistance the body has to malnourishment and infectious disease. Pre-revolutionary Cuba ranked third out of 11 Latin American countries in per capita daily caloric consumption. Cuba ranks lower than the same countries today.

Education

Castro likes to cite education as a triumph of the revolution. Cuba's literacy rate is 96 percent, second only to Argentina in Latin America. Although this is an impressive statistic, improvement in education is not unique to Castro's revolution. For example, Cuba had been among the most literate countries in Latin America since before the revolution. It ranked fourth in the 1950s. Moreover, Panama and Colombia, which ranked behind Cuba in literacy rates at the time, has matched Cuba's improvement in terms of percentage.

Cuba provides free education to all children and adults. The school year runs from the first week of September to the first week of July. Primary grades are for students aged 6 to 11. Students at ages 12 to 18 attend secondary schools. There are two levels to secondary schools. All students at ages from 12 to 15 years old attend basic secondary school and take the same courses. Upon completing this basic level, students must take "placement" examinations to determine the types of courses they will take at ages 16 to 18 to finish secondary school.

Some students will finish their secondary schooling by attending "technical" schools that train them for jobs as skilled workers (such as mechanics, machinists, and chemists) and middle-level technicians (such as factory managers). After graduation, these students may choose to attend technological institutes for advanced training. Other students qualify for "upper secondary" schools that prepare them for entrance into universities.

Graduation from an upper secondary school does not guarantee admission to a university. Admission is gained partly by the applicant's attitude toward the revolution and the student's participation in Communist youth organizations. Students that enter universities do not choose their major programs. They take entrance examinations and are assigned a program based on their intellectual strengths. The state denies some fields of study, such as the social sciences, to students that do not show enough interest in achieving the goals of the revolution. University graduates are eligible for jobs in such areas as medicine, engineering, and teaching.

Cuba also has sports academies. Cuba copied its sports academy system from the former Soviet Union, which excelled in training athletes for the Olympic games. The sports academies have the same structure as the primary and secondary schools, except that only students that show athletic talent attend the academies. The academies teach all subjects but focus on sports in a scientific way to develop the students' bodies.

The Cuban education system emphasizes indoctrination of Communist theory at all levels. Children are required to participate in political activities. For example, school buses took students in Havana directly from school to join mass demonstrations in the city to call for the return to Cuba of the six-year-old boy Elián Gonzáles.

The government uses an educational system that requires students to live away from home in boarding schools for part of the school year. The state requires older primary school students to spend at least one month a year away from home working in agriculture. Most secondary students must live in boarding schools the entire year. They spend half their time working in the fields. Amnesty International, an organization devoted to promoting human rights, criticizes this practice by calling it an excuse by the state to use children as a source of free labor. Pope John Paul II criticized this practice during his visit to Cuba in January 1998.

Communications Media

Granma, named for the boat that Castro and his men used to invade the island in 1956, is the official newspaper of the Communist Party and the country's main source of news. Weekly editions of *Granma* are available abroad in French,

English, and Spanish. An abbreviated multilingual version titled *Granma International* is accessible on the Internet at *www.granma.cu*. Each province publishes a newspaper detailing local news. The government censors the articles in these newspapers. An Internet site titled CubaNet, founded by Cuban-Americans in Miami, publishes uncensored news about Cuban politics and daily life. Independent press agencies and freelance writers based in Cuba provide this news, which is accessed at *www.cubanet.org/cubanews.html*.

Cuba was the first country in Latin America to have a radio broadcasting station. The first broadcast was in 1918, and regular programming began in 1922. About 100 radio stations broadcast in Cuba now. The stations are divided into five national networks and five provincial networks. The state controls all programming, which is set up for cultural and educational programs to foster the goals of the revolution. For example, Radio Rebelde (a national network) offers Russian-language instruction as well as literary and political commentary. The United States operates Radio Martí in southern Florida to counter some of the Cuban government's political rhetoric.

There are three television stations in Cuba—two in Havana, named Televisora Nacional, and one in Santiago de Cuba, named Tele-Rebelde. One of the Havana stations is educational; it broadcasts programs in science, language, and mathematics. The other is also cultural and educational, but includes entertainment. It is common to see old movies and recent dramas from Cuba and other countries.

Weights and Measures, Time, and Holidays

Cuba uses the metric system rather than English system of weights and measures. Grams and kilograms appear on packages, not ounces and pounds. Meters and kilometers designate distances, not feet and miles. Hectares reference areas, not acres.

Cuba keeps the same daily time that the U.S. East Coast does, which is Eastern Standard Time. The island is five hours behind Greenwich mean time (or universal time coordinates). If it is 3 P.M. in Havana, it will be 8 P.M. in Greenwich, England. Additionally, as in the United States, Cuba is on daylight savings time from about the beginning of spring to the end of fall, during which Cuba is only four hours behind Greenwich, England. As a result, Cubans turn their clocks an hour forward in late March ("spring forward") and an hour backward at the beginning of October ("fall back").

Cubans celebrate five holidays, when most shops, offices, and museums are closed. They celebrate Liberation Day on January 1, which recalls January 1, 1959, when Batista fled the island and rebel forces, represented by Che Guevara, entered Havana. National Rebellion Day, May 1, celebrates the July 26, 1953, attack by Castro on the army barracks in Santiago de Cuba in the hopes of sparking a popular uprising. On this day, Cubans gather at the Plaza de la Revolucin (Plaza of the Revolution) in Havana to hear Castro speak. The Day of Cuban Culture marks the beginning of the First War of Independence on October 10, 1868. Christmas, December 25, celebrates the birth of Christ. This holiday was banished by the Castro government in the early 1970s, because it interfered with the sugarcane harvest. However, Castro reinstated Christmas as a holiday as a gesture of goodwill when Pope John Paul II visited Cuba in 1998.

On other days, Cubans commemorate various other things, but these are not public holidays. For example, they recognize the birthday of José Martí (January 28), International Women's Day (March 8), Children's Day (April 4), the victory at the Bay of Pigs (April 19), Mother's Day (second Sunday in May), Father's Day (third Sunday in June), and the death of Che Guevara (October 8).

Citizens leave Cuba illegally in makeshift boats and head toward Florida in search of better societal and economic conditions.

Conclusion

Admirers of Cuba often call this island nation the "Pearl of the Antilles" because of its beautiful natural and cultural landscapes and its potential riches. In the modern world, Cuba should be a center of trade and wealth due to its favorable geographical location and varied natural resource base. However, the country's history has not complemented its geography. Cuba has never enjoyed true political independence, and it has degenerated into one of the poorest countries in Latin America.

The advantage of geographical location has entwined Cuba with the United States economically and politically for more than a century. The U.S. involvement in Cuba began with American businessmen financing Cuban agriculture and it grew with the intervention of U.S. troops in the Cuban Second War of Independence. Cuba was a republic from 1902 to 1959, but in name only. This period was a cycle of internal corruption, dictatorship, and U.S. military intervention. When Castro overthrew Batista in 1959, hopes were high among many Cubans and Americans that Cuba would break this cycle and finally begin to realize its full potential. However, Castro turned out to be another dictator and Cuba's economy became dependent on subsidies from the Soviet Union.

By 1962, after Castro had confiscated American property, made alliances with the Soviet Union, and pledged to spread revolution throughout Latin America and Africa, relations with the United States soured. President Kennedy imposed a trade embargo that continues today.

When the Cold War ended, many imagined that there would be a warming of relations between these former enemies. However, the large exiled Cuban-American community in the United States has a powerful lobby in Washington, D.C. As a result, during the 1990s, the U.S. Congress passed two laws (the Cuba Democracy Act and the Helms-Burton Act) that strengthened the U.S. trade embargo.

Both countries now seem willing to share in a policy of cautious engagement. U.S. presidents have chosen not to enforce the harshest terms of the Helms-Burton Act; Castro's response to the visit of Pope John Paul II has had a positive effect on relations between the two countries; and the United States recently made its first shipment of food and medicine to Cuba in 40 years. In May 2002, former U.S. President Jimmy Carter visited Cuba and received a warm welcome.

Castro's popularity has waned in recent years as the Cuban economy has hit on hard times. The most basic essentials of living—food, fuel, and housing—are scarce. The government's handling of these shortages—ration cards, blackouts, and resettlement—is inadequate. The basic aspects of the nation's infrastructure—public transportation, garbage collection, homes, buildings, water supply, electricity, and even military equipment—are crumbling. By means of a lottery, the government allows tens of thousands of Cubans to leave the island

Pope John Paul II made a historic visit to Cuba in January 1998. He celebrated masses outdoors and met with Fidel Castro to encourage him to allow more religious and political freedom.

each year. Hundreds of thousands more are waiting for the lottery to choose them. Thousands more are trying to escape illegally each year, as well. Capitalistic reforms, although minor, are tacit admissions that socialism has been a failure.

Cuba is clearly at a critical juncture in its history, and change seems inevitable. Outside observers are asking three questions about Cuba's future. The first question is "When will Cuba abandon socialism?" As a whole, Cubans still support Castro for his charisma. Most Cubans refer to him as "Fidel." Many homes still conspicuously display his photograph with the popular phrase "*Fidel esta es tu casa*" (Fidel, this is your home). When receiving something free, it is still customary for many Cubans to respond by saying "*Gracias Fidel*" (Thank you Fidel).

Castro holds so much power within Cuban society, the Communist Party, and the government that he must be the one to call for the abandonment of socialism. However, the bearded leader's speeches indicate that he is not going to do that. Lamentably, until Castro gives up the reins of power or dies, Cubans will continue to wake in the morning and ask broodingly, "What am I going to eat today?"

A second question that outside observers of Cuba are asking is "Who will end up running a post-Castro Cuba?" Castro is, after all, 76 years old. No one knows for sure the answer to this question. Fidel's brother Raúl is 5 years younger than Fidel and is constitutionally in line to replace him. Despite his younger age, Raúl's health does not appear to be any better than Fidel's. Unlike his older brother, Raúl tends to shun the limelight, so analysts know little about how or how long he would lead. One can only speculate what Cuba would be like under Raúl Castro. Moreover, given his age, analysts are already speculating about which of Cuba's younger Communist leaders would succeed him.

The third question that outside experts are asking is "Given an imminent change in leadership, should the United States reduce economic sanctions against Cuba?" The Cuban-American lobby argues that easing the embargo will only help Cuban Communism and its socialist economy survive. They say that Fidel's having to make capitalistic adjustments is proof that the embargo is finally beginning to work.

Lawmakers representing agricultural and tourism interests are seeking new markets. They have led the charge to ease the trade embargo. Additionally, many well-respected former U.S. politicians and former government officials are urging a policy shift. They argue that Castro's capitalistic adjustments have more to do with the loss of Soviet subsidies than the U.S. trade embargo. The embargo, they say, is punishing the Cuban people, not the Cuban leadership. They believe that commerce, trade, and visitation by Americans and others who know freedom is the best way to bring about change in Cuba.

Facts at a Glance

Physical Geography

Total Area 42,803 square miles (110,860 square kilometers)

Climate Tropical; moderated by trade winds; dry season (November to April); rainy season (May to October)

Terrain Mostly flat to rolling plains, with rugged hills and mountains in some areas

Highest Point Pico Turquino 6,576 feet (2,005 meters)

Natural Resources Nickel, cobalt, iron ore, copper, manganese, silica, petroleum, arable land

Land Use Arable land, 24 percent; permanent crops, 7 percent; permanent pastures, 27 percent; forests and woodland, 24 percent; other, 18 percent

Irrigated Land 3,514 square miles (9,100 square kilometers)

Natural Hazards Hurricanes from August to October; droughts

People

Population 11,184,023 (2001 estimate)

Population Growth Rate 0.37 percent

Net Migration Rate -1.36 migrant(s)/1,000 population

Life Expectancy at Birth 76.4 years

Ethnic Groups Mulatto, 51 percent; white, 37 percent; black, 11 percent; Chinese, 1 percent

Religions Nominally 85 percent Roman Catholic prior to Castro assuming power; Protestants, Jehovah's Witnesses, Jews, and Santería are also represented

Language Spanish

Literacy 95.7 percent

Government

Government Type Communist state

Capital Havana

Administrative Divisions 14 provinces and 1 special municipality

Economy

GDP	$19.2 billion
Labor Force by Occupation	Agriculture, 25 percent; industry, 24 percent; services, 51 percent
Industries	Sugar, petroleum, tobacco, chemicals, construction, services, nickel, steel, cement
Agricultural Products	Sugar, tobacco, citrus, coffee, rice, potatoes, beans, livestock
Export Commodities	Sugar, nickel, tobacco, fish, medical products, citrus, coffee
Exports—Main Partners	Russia, the Netherlands, Canada, Spain
Import Commodities	Petroleum, food, machinery, chemicals, semifinished goods, transport equipment, consumer goods
Imports—Main Partners	Spain, Venezuela, Canada, France

History at a Glance

3000 B.C.E.	Approximate date of arrival of the first the Indians on the island of Cuba.
1492	Columbus lands on Cuba and claims it as a possession of Spain.
1511–1515	Diego de Velázquez leads a ruthless conquest of the Indians and the early settlement of Cuba.
1868–1878	First War of Independence.
1895–1898	Second War of Independence.
1898	U.S. forces aid Cuba rebels during the last year of the Second War of Independence. Historians refer to this phase of the war as the Spanish-American War.
1898–1902	U.S. forces occupy Cuba until the Cubans create a republic.
1901	United States enacts the Platt Amendment.
1902	Cuban people elect Tomás Estrada Palma as the first president of the Republic of Cuba. He serves two four-year terms.
1903	Under the terms of the Platt Amendment, a U.S. naval station is established at Guantánamo Bay.
1924–1933	Gerardo Machado is president of Cuba.
1933–1958	Fulgencio Batista controls Cuba.
1953	Fidel Castro attacks the Moncada military barracks in Santiago de Cuba.
1956	Fidel Castro establishes guerrilla operations in the Sierra Maestra of southeastern Cuba.
1959	Fulgencio Batista relinquishes power and flees the country. Fidel Castro becomes prime minister.
1960	Cuban government nationalizes U.S. businesses and properties. The United States responds by breaking off diplomatic relations and begins a partial trade embargo on Cuba.
1960–1983	Cuban government involved in training revolutionary groups and sending Cuban troops to fight "wars of liberation" in Latin America and Africa.

1961 United States bans all U.S. trade with Cuba. The Bay of Pigs invasion fails and Fidel Castro declares that he is a true believer of Communism.

1962 Cuban Missile Crisis occurs.

1965 Cuba forms the Communist Party and its government officially becomes communist.

1967 Ernesto "Che" Guevara leads a band of rebels in Bolivia. The Bolivian military captures and executes him.

1980 Castro starts the Mariel boatlift by announcing that 135,000 Cubans can illegally depart for the United States. Many Cubans try to cross the Straits of Florida on rickety boats and drown.

1983 U.S. forces invade Grenada to prevent Cuba from building an airfield; the Americans kill a large number of Cuban soldiers defending the airfield.

1991 Former Soviet Union breaks up. As a result, Cuba's economy begins to suffer severe shortages of food, fuel, and other products.

1992 United States enacts the Cuba Democracy Act, which prevents foreign businesses owned by U.S. companies from trading with Cuba. It also allows Cuban Americans to visit relatives in Cuba once a year.

1994 Cubans riot in the streets of Havana due to food and fuel shortages; the Cuban government responds by allowing Cubans to leave the country in homemade boats.

1996 Cuban military shoots down two U.S. registered civil aircraft, killing three U.S. citizens and one U.S. resident. In response, the U.S. Helms-Burton Act authorizes the president to impose trade sanctions on other countries that trade with Cuba or that use confiscated U.S. properties in Cuba.

1998 Pope John Paul II visits Cuba for five days. In response to his visit, the United States allows Americans to visit Cuba under certain circumstances. Castro responds by declaring Christmas a national holiday.

1999–2000   U.S. fishing boat rescues Elián González from a shipwreck that killed his mother. They were fleeing Cuba. After a 7-month legal battle, the United States returns the boy to Cuba to live with his father.

2000   United States modifies its trade sanctions to allow trade with Cuba in agricultural commodities, medicine, and medical supplies, as long the purchaser is not controlled, owned, or operated by the Cuban government.

2001   The first American ship to dock in Cuba in almost 40 years arrives in Havana with a shipment of food and medicine from the United States.

Agromercado: Farmers market in which farmers set prices in U.S. dollars.

Arawak: The main group of Indians inhabiting Cuba when the Spaniards arrived on the island.

Bodega: A state-run store to which Cubans take ration cards for food items and consumer goods.

Bohió: The thatch-roofed house of rural peasant.

Cayo: Spanish Caribbean word for cay or key, a low coral island.

Casas particulares: Privately operated bed and breakfasts.

Cha-cha: A semi-fast ballroom dance invented in Cuba that descended from the son.

Cuba Libre: Literal meaning is free Cuba. Cubans used this phrase as a battle cry and political slogan during their wars of independence. It is now the name of a drink made with rum and Coca-Cola.

Cuban trogon: The national bird of Cuba.

Criollos: White Spaniards born in the colony.

Cold War: A war (1945-1991) of hostile diplomacy, intrigue, and subversion between Communist and non-Communist countries.

Fidelismo: A popular term used by Cubans to describe Fidel Castro's personal brand of socialism.

Finca: A coffee plantation; usually a small, family-owned occupied farm.

Granma: The name of the yacht used by Castro to invade Cuba in 1956. Granma Province was named after the yacht.

Greater Antilles: Cuba, Hispaniola, Puerto Rico, and Jamaica.

Gross domestic product: A measure of economic growth: the value of all final goods and services produced within a country in a given year.

Guayabera: Literal meaning is guava picker. A starched white shirt of linen or cotton, ribbed and decorated with buttons.

Harbor: A sheltered bay where ships are safe from storms.

Glossary

Hoyo: Literal meaning hole or pit. Spanish word for sinkhole, a saucer-shaped depression in karst areas.

Isla: Spanish word for island.

Karst: Slavic name of a limestone area in Slovenia, a country in Eastern Europe. Geologists use it to describe limestone areas where most or all of the drainage is by underground channels and surface features include sinkholes, etc.

Libretas: A ration card issued by the government of Cuba.

Mulatto: A person of black and white ancestry

Santería: Afro-Cuban religion that combines Catholic and Yoruba traditions.

Marxist-Leninist socialism: An extreme form of socialism that advocates state ownership and control of all means of production and single political party (the Communist Party) rule.

Massif: French word for a general mountainous area that breaks up into peaks toward the summit and has relatively uniform characteristics.

Mogotes: Steep-sided, cone-shaped hills in karst areas.

Orisha: An Afro-Cuban god or spirit.

Paladares: Privately operated family restaurants.

Pico: Spanish word for peak.

Revolution, The: The creation of a socialist system that brings forth a classless Communist society.

Royal palm tree: National tree of Cuba.

Salsa: Music that is a mixture of jazz, the Cuban son, and other Latin rhythms.

Sierra: Spanish word for mountain range.

Son: The first music to mix well Spanish lyrics with African rhythm. The son gave rise to other forms of Afro-Cuban music, such as the rumba, conga, mambo, and cachucha.

Sabana: Arawak word for grassland.

Subsidy: A grant of money to prop up a government or a particular business.

Casa de tobacco: Literal meaning is tobacco house. It is a shed used to store and dry tobacco leaves.

Vega: A tobacco farm.

Yoruba: A Nigerian African tribe.

Bibliography

Aeberhard, Danny, ed. *Insight Guide:Cuba*. Maspeth, NY: Langenscheidt Publishers, Inc., 2000.

Black, Jan Knippers, et al. 2 ed. *Area Handbook for Cuba*. Washington, D.C.: U.S. Government Printing Office, 1976.

Central Intelligence Agency. *CIA Fact Book*. Washington, D.C.: U.S. Government Printing Office, 2001.

CubaNet. Cuba news. (*www.cubanet.org/cubanews.html*). Accessed various dates, February-March, 2002.

Dana, Jr. Richard Henry. *To Cuba and Back*. (Reprint) Carbondale, IL: Southern Illinois University Press, 1966.

González Echevarría, Roberto. *The Pride of Havana: A History of Cuban Baseball*. New York: Oxford University Press, 1999.

Government of Cuba. Granma International (*www.granma.cu*). Accessed various dates, February-March, 2002.

Government of India. Embassy of India, Havana (Cuba) (*www.indembassyhavana.cu*). Last update December 7, 2001.

Greene, Graham. *Our Man in Havana*. Willam Heinemann Ltd., 1958.

Hemingway, Ernest. *The Old Man and the Sea*. C. Scribner's Sons, 1952.

Hinckle, Warren and Turner, William. *The Fish Is Red: The Story of the Secret War Against Castro*. New York: Harper and Row Publishers, 1981.

Hostetter, Martha, ed. *Cuba*. New York: H.W. Wilson Company, 2001.

Hunt, Howard. *Give Us This Day*. New Rochelle, NY: Arlington House, 1973.

Luis, William. *Culture and Customs of Cuba*. Westport, CN: Greenwood Press, 2001.

MacGaffey, Wyatt and Barnett, Clifford R. *Cuba: its people, its society, its culture*. New Haven, CN: Human Relations Area Files, Inc., 1962.

Marrero y Artiles, Levi. 2 ed. *Geografía de Cuba*. New York: Minerva Books, Ltd., 1970.

Michener, James A. and Kings, John. *Six Days in Havana*. Austin, TX: University of Texas Press, 1989.

Moses, Catherine. *Real Life in Castro's Cuba*. Wilmington, DE: Scholarly Resources, Inc., 2000.

Pérez Jr., Louis A. *Cuba: Between Reform and Revolution*. New York: Oxford University Press, 1988.

Pérez Jr., Louis A. *On Becoming Cuban: Identity, Nationality, and Culture*. Chapel Hill, NC: University of North Carolina Press, 1999.

Pérez Jr., Louis A. *Winds of Change: Hurricanes and the Transformation of Nineteenth-Century Cuba*. Chapel Hill, NC: University of North Carolina Press, 2001.

Stanley, David. 2 ed. *Cuba*. Footscray, Victoria, Australia: Lonely Planet Publications, 2000.

U.S. Department of State. Cuba: Country Report on Human Rights Practices—2001 (*http://www.state.gov/g/drl/rls/hrrpt/2001/wha/8333.htm*). Accessed March 5, 2002.

von Humboldt, Alexander. *Personal Narrative of Travels to the Equinoctial Regions of the New Continent, During the Years 1799-1804*. (Reprint) New York: AMS Press, Inc., 1966.

West, Robert C. and Aguelli, John P. 3 ed. *Middle America: Its Lands and Peoples*. Englewood Cliffs, NJ: Prentice-Hall, Inc., 1989.

Index

Index

Picture Credits

DR. RICHARD A. CROOKER is a geography professor at Kutztown University in Pennsylvania, where he teaches physical geography, oceanography, map reading, and climatology. He received a Ph.D. in geography from the University of California, Riverside. Dr. Crooker is a member of the Association of American Geographers and the National Council for Geographic Education. He has received numerous research grants, including three from the National Geographical Society. His publications deal with a wide range of geographical topics. He enjoys reading, hiking, bicycling, kayaking, and boogie boarding.

CHARLES F. "FRITZ" GRITZNER is Distinguished Professor of Geography at South Dakota State University. He is now in his fifth decade of college teaching and research. Much of his career work has focused on geographic education. Fritz has served as both president and executive director of the National Council for Geographic Education and has received the Council's George J. Miller Award for Distinguished Service.